IN
DEFENCE
OF
WEALTH

{ A MODEST REBUTTAL
TO THE CHARGE THE RICH
ARE BAD FOR SOCIETY }

IN
DEFENCE
OF
WEALTH

DEREK BULLEN

BARLOW BOOKS
fine books for enterprising authors

Text copyright © Derek Bullen, 2022

Library and Archives Canada Cataloguing in Publication data available
upon request.

978-1-988025-70-4 (hardcover)

Printed in Canada

Publisher: Sarah Scott
Book producer: Tracy Bordian/At Large Editorial Services
Cover design: Paul Hodgson
Interior design and layout: Rob Scanlan
Copy editing: Eleanor Gasparik
Proofreading: Wendy Thomas
Indexing: Karen Hunter

For more information, visit **www.barlowbooks.com**

**BARLOW
BOOKS**

Barlow Book Publishing Inc.
96 Elm Avenue, Toronto, ON
Canada M4W 1P2

CONTENTS

INTRODUCTION

I am a one-percenter.

Wow. That must be so nice.

I get it. What could I possibly complain about?

A kind of social cold war has been declared on wealth. Wealth is being scapegoated for every problem, from climate change to poverty to inadequate child care for working moms. The argument goes like this: The wealthy aren't paying their fair share! The wealthy have too much influence! The wealthy are elitist! The wealthy are lazy! They don't give back. They're ungrateful and privileged. And think of it: taxing all that wealth could fund important social programs to protect the vulnerable and pay off government debt. It's politically expedient and increasingly popular among so-called progressives not just in Canada but also in the United States, the United Kingdom, France, Germany, Australia, and New Zealand to demonize the wealthy.

I wrote *In Defence of Wealth* for one simple reason: we want more rich people, not fewer. We want more successful entrepreneurs, not fewer. We need more risk takers, more wealth creators. The standard

1

of living we enjoy in the developed world is the consequence of wealth creation.

I grew up in a lower-income working-class section of Calgary, where the few who made it out were blackballed as traitors to their class. My dad was one of them. I am a self-made millionaire, but it took me twenty-eight years to get here. People don't see the risk, sacrifice, hard work, and long hours required to make it. They don't see what it takes to create wealth or how wealth benefits everyone when it is created. Or don't want to see.

Every time someone decries a company for making money, they are totally oblivious to the casualties who tried and failed, or succeeded but could not hang on. Google is making tons of dough, yes. But what about Yahoo or AltaVista? Facebook is being raked over the coals for being too successful, but who remembers Myspace, Nextopia, or AOL? Before Netflix took over the world there was … Blockbuster. Amazon is thriving, but what about eToys.com, Global Crossing, HomeGrocer. com? They were touted as world-beaters too. Microsoft succeeded but somewhere in the weeds are Netscape, Borland, Lotus Software, and WordPerfect.

Elon Musk founded Tesla Motors in 2003 and, having improbably survived a soap-opera series of existential ups and downs, has almost single-handedly revolutionized the automobile industry. Does anyone stop and wonder how? Does anyone appreciate the risks Musk took? Or appreciate and admire his protean stamina against unfathomably long odds?

Real people, real investors, real pension funds put their time and money likewise into the investments that didn't win. I believe CEOs who have built something fantastic and enduring are the professional athletes of the business world. They are skilled, invested, willing to take risks to get ahead, focused on the game both during office hours and personal time—and doing it all in front of others. CEOs are stars in the top percentile of the game of business. The CEOs that made it and continually evolve to stay in the game—Gates, Bezos, Zuckerberg—are like sports legends. And, yes, unlike the mob gathered at the castle gates, I believe they have earned their wealth.

I can tell you from experience that not one of the politicians or pundits who argues about how highly paid successful CEOs are—how unfair it is and how they never pay their fair share—ever dropped by with some reassuring words or sage advice when a CEO was sweating deep into the night over how to come up with payroll or when a bank suddenly cut off a line of credit.

Welcome to *In Defence of Wealth*.

In the following pages, we consider some of the commonly held assumptions about wealth. We consider the main critique: the more that rich people have, the less everyone else has. We examine the key themes in popular media: Are the rich paying their fair share? Is poverty increasing as the number of millionaires goes up? Should governments tax the wealthiest members of society out of existence? The lion's share of this book is devoted to the fact-based proof that these assumptions driving the critique of the rich are wrong.

To be clear: I am more comfortable creating wealth than I am critiquing it. I am not a historian, nor am I an economist or an academic. I do believe, however, that what I lack in study of wealth creation from a safe and comfortable, risk-free distance, I make up for in practical hands-on experience as an entrepreneur and CEO for more than thirty years. *In Defence of Wealth* is about wealth creation as I have lived it and understand it, and what that means to all of us. It is the product of my perspective and my experience. It is my story, and the story of others who made a lot more money in their lifetimes than I have, and how it came to benefit us all. We will explore the evidence supporting the thesis that wealth is not the enemy, but the solution.

While I hope at least a few readers will agree with me, I fully expect many will not. In fact, I welcome all objections. However, it needs to be understood what is being defended, and what is not. I do mean to defend wealth creation, but I am not making a blanket defence of the system itself. I don't defend laziness, greed, or shady practices. I support policy that makes it easier for as many as possible to climb the ladder of financial self-sufficiency; I am against anything that stifles real competition. Competition is good—for people, companies, countries, and for society. I also believe a free market is better than governments at helping people work their way to the top—and that we all benefit in the process. The job of government is to keep the playing field level.

Wealth does not make a person good. However— and this is more to the point—neither does wealth necessarily make a person bad. Frankly, I am not sure that is at all obvious.

{ CHAPTER 1 }

MY STORY

Whenever I hear about "the rich" being hunted in the media or in some political circles, I ask a simple question: where would we all be without our wealth? I don't mean wealthy people; I mean all of us. Where does all this bounty come from? Do we ever wonder who creates new wealth?

Put-downs and assumptions about "really rich guys" can make it sound like we are causing every problem, from the high cost of housing, climate change, and student debt to the fact that the Leafs haven't won the Stanley Cup in more than fifty years. Worse, that we are accused of getting rich on the backs of everyone else. The put-downs are endlessly repeated. We lack empathy and don't care about the poor, and our elevated status makes it impossible for us to connect with others. We don't deserve our wealth, and we aren't paying our fair share. When we contribute to a charity, the line goes, we do it only because we want to get a tax receipt. It all makes popular press and popular politics, but is it true?

Let's start at the beginning, with the belief that rich people don't deserve their wealth. In the same way that a legend like Michael Jordan spent an insane amount of thought, practice, and discipline in becoming the heart and soul of a winning NBA dynasty, an entrepreneur who desires to create wealth for himself or the community must dedicate wild amounts of time and focus on his pursuit. It isn't for everyone: it's a lot of work and there are risks. Just as one injury can stop an elite athlete's career, fatal injuries in business can end the whole dream in the blink of an eye. Critics of the rich overlook this critical truth: it is extremely hard to build wealth in the first place and even harder to keep it.

Every successful entrepreneur has hit the panic button multiple times. Tom Jenkins, chair of the board at OpenText Corporation, which specializes in enterprise information management software, learned a painful lesson in the late 1990s when the company was a major player in the business of search engines. This was before Google became a major player. "When we announced that we were no longer going to be the search engine for Yahoo!, the stock market reaction was immediate and severe," Jenkins wrote later. Within six months, the company's stock price plummeted from $20 a share to $2. "When you take the garbage out to the end of your driveway and realize that many of the homes you see belong to people who lost a good chunk of their money because of your failure, it's very personal and very painful," Jenkins wrote in an essay about the experience in the book *Canadian Failures: Stories of Building Success* (Dundurn Press, 2017).

Sir James Dyson spent fifteen years trying 5,126 different iterations of what would eventually become the Dual Cyclone vacuum cleaner, which came on the market in 1993. In a 2012 conversation with the website Entrepreneur, he noted that failure is a crucial part of making progress. "You never learn from success, but you do learn from failure," he said. "I got to a place I never could have imagined because I learned what worked and didn't work."

My own story is another example of how hard it is to found and grow a business.

I grew up in a working-class Calgary neighbourhood. It was all right, as far as I was concerned. I had a lot of friends. It was a nice and friendly street where everyone knew everyone else, and we all got along and had fun. It was great. Back then most of all the dads had blue-collar jobs. Most had never been to college, and a few had barely made it through high school. My dad was the exception, with an engineering degree. He grew up very poor in Medicine Hat, Alberta, where he was home-schooled to grade nine and became the second in his family to go to and graduate university. My dad studied hard in high school to earn a scholarship and made the money to stay in university by working as a carpenter framing houses each summer. He was an incredibly hard worker.

Most of the other dads in the neighbourhood headed off to work in the morning and came home at night to crack a beer, relax on the couch, watch hockey on TV, and go to bed. My dad was rarely around in the evenings to watch TV or toss a football; he was often working.

He worked for an oilfield services company during the day. When he came home, he changed clothes and worked as a carpenter most nights and weekends. My mother, meanwhile, gave up her job as a nurse to be a full-time homemaker and take care of my two brothers and me.

My father's after-hours work in carpentry paid off. He did a framing job for a man who turned out to be his future partner in what would become the enormously successful company Canadian Fracmaster.

It wasn't long after my father started with Canadian Fracmaster that we moved to a bigger house in a better neighbourhood. My dad built the house we moved into. I was ten. Few of our friends seemed happy for us. We had hit the lottery; we were on our way out. Lucky us, right? There was bitter resentment from our old neighbours. We were no longer part of the community we grew up in. It seemed unfair to them that we, and not they, were rich.

What they didn't acknowledge, of course, was how hard my father worked, the many years he worked double shifts, or the sacrifices he made.

There's the rub. A lot of us don't want to look beneath the varnish. All we see is the shine. Most of us want the rewards, but we don't want the hard work and sacrifice success requires.

It's common these days to talk a lot about opportunity—"we need to create more opportunity for our young people"—as if opportunity were a magical resource that pours open on demand. It isn't even close to being that easy, and we do entrepreneurs a huge disservice to pretend it is.

Anyway, back to the Bullens in the 1970s. Suddenly we were surrounded by families with parents who were lawyers, doctors, businessmen, and hoteliers. The kids all talked about going to university and having their own careers. That didn't make me any happier. I had lost my friends from the old neighbourhood and had few new friends in the new neighbourhood, and my parents had started the first stage of a toxic marital meltdown. Money doesn't create these issues; it just magnifies them.

When I went to university, I came into my own. I played in a band and earned my own money. I bought one of the first synthesizers on the market. I was in a new wave band, and we packed the local clubs and bars. We cut a record with three songs that climbed the local charts, making it into the top 100 on local AM and FM stations in 1983.

I was learning to work hard for what I wanted, and I have kept that ethic my whole life. It's essential for me.

TOP OF THE WORLD ... TO BOTTOMING OUT

Fast-forward to 1990. I had graduated as an electrical engineer, dropped the band, and been working as a computer programmer and consultant out of Calgary. I had married my wife, Susan, and we had two of our three children, Brittany and Tessa, and a house with two mortgages at 12.5 percent that we couldn't really afford. Then I met my father's new financial partner, who offered me an incredible opportunity to develop a new digitizing software they could use to get an attractive grant from the government of Ireland. I was twenty-nine years old—moving to Ireland to work on new technology sounded like a lottery win to me. I was given equity in the company, and I was making a good salary during my time in Ireland. Of course, we weren't saving a dime. We were having too much fun.

Then I got fired. The dream was over in less than five minutes. Literally twelve months to the day after we first arrived. I will never forget it. One day the senior partner showed up and informed me that I no longer had a seat with the company. I had clashed with the president of the company over the technology platform on which we should develop our digitization software. I was out—with no severance and the shares I owned were made worthless.

I was stunned! What was going on? What happened? The next three or four days were a confusing blur. I couldn't eat; I couldn't sleep—it was like being seasick on dry land. The girls were too young to understand, of course, but my wife was amazingly strong and patient. She has always been superb in a crisis. We packed up and moved back to Canada, with barely enough cash to buy our plane tickets. It was a sobering comedown. We managed to save a few pieces of essential furniture, but the rest we were forced to give away as we simply couldn't afford the expense of shipping it. Plus, we had no place to send it to. We had leased out our Calgary home before the move. We ended up staying with my mother, who was living alone at the time, having recently divorced my father. My mother was less than thrilled with the new domestic arrangements, and—no surprise—it took no time at all for us to wear out our welcome. So we moved in with my in-laws.

My in-laws, Elliot and Alberta, were gracious and generous, and made it clear that we could stay with them as long as we needed. However, they had recently downsized to a smaller house, and the added burden of suddenly accommodating two adults and two grandchildren was, we realized, unfair on them.

In what turned out to be a surreal two-year period that made me think of author Douglas Adams's book *The Long Dark Tea-Time of the Soul,* we moved eleven times to cheaper and cheaper housing. It took me quite some time not to wince at the sight of a suitcase. Each move seemed smaller, shabbier, and more depressing than the previous one. It was like tipping dominos in a game of downward mobility.

Back on the street, with no savings, no job, no income, no place to stay, and two young children, the situation was bleak. What a shocking loss it had been. What had seemed an incredibly promising future had crashed overnight. I was back to square one. Actually, worse than square one. I had a wife and family to support. And no means of support. We were "home" without a home. We needed cash and figured it might be easier if my wife asked for a line of credit from our bank for cash to live on. She didn't mention that I had been fired and had no job, but luckily the rules were less strict back then and my career status was never checked.

Success is exhilarating. But in my experience, in sheer emotional magnitude, nothing compares to the momentum of failure. It is terrible, hopeless, frightening, and soul-crushing. It's been my experience—and it's singularly fundamental to my argument—that failure, the constant and ever-present risk of failure, is a motivating factor of wealth creation that no one judging from the outside ever sees or even accepts as real. No, I'm not talking about the normal, mostly annoying setbacks we all confront; I'm talking nuclear-magnitude disaster. The kind of existential threat where you find yourself staring into the dark maw of the abyss and realize there might be no way back. I've encountered several of those occasions, and they're not fun. If you have built your own business, you know exactly what I am talking about.

"Maybe you should just take a regular job," my wife suggested one evening as we sat at our tiny kitchen table after the girls had gone to sleep. We were at a low point in our apartment-hopping period. It's not that I hadn't considered it.

"If I work for someone else, they're just going to end up firing me," I countered. I tend to make moves that are not obvious in the short term but prove to be the right thing in the long term. Back in the early 1990s, for instance, I could see that clunky DEC mainframe computers, with their green text-only screens, would become obsolete in the face of powerful new computers from companies like Sun Microsystems with graphical interfaces and monumental computing power. This had been the source of my dispute with the company president in Ireland in 1991. It was obvious to me at the time, but it would take a few years for the company that fired me to realize the same thing. So as bad as our circumstances seemed, I truly believed that building my own company, and making it work, was the only option in front of me for long-term success.

It was one of the most terrifying moments of my life, albeit an incredible challenge to lean into. While the exhilaration was indescribable, it was also around this time that one of my daughters began packing up her clothes every night in little brown lunch bags before going to bed. We asked her what she was doing.

"If we move again, I don't want to forget anything."

In those days, finding talent for a new computer-related project was done old-school. Companies wanting to hire would place ads in newspapers, resumés were sent via courier or fax, prospecting was done in the Yellow Pages, clients deputized receptionists to screen calls, e-mail existed but was not widely used, and networks and data storage were both rudimentary.

I saw an opportunity to provide computer professionals on demand. Our first slice at a mission statement was to provide on-demand software developers for the oil and gas industry. It was a great concept, and I would move from a small volunteer operation into one that employs 3,500 people and generates half a billion dollars of revenue a year. Over the years we were able to broaden our expertise across numerous industries and geographies. There were a lot of potholes along the road, but I am proud to say that we never abandoned or in any way compromised our commitment to four foundational principles:

we would be accountable, transparent, professional, and driven.

At the beginning, we needed a name. I dusted off a company name I had come up with a few years earlier while watching a James Bond movie, *A View to a Kill.* I noticed that Sharper Image had a product placement in the film. It seemed like a cool name for a company: Sharper Image Oil and Gas Systems. My first smart move was realizing that typing out the company name hundreds of times a day was taking up huge chunks of time. I shortened it to S.i. Systems.

In the first decade, growing my business was an endless cycle of investing, losing money temporarily, clawing our way back into the black, tumbling into the red, only to repeat the same process again and again.

I started the company in 1991 with an office in a super-low-rent area under the railway tracks in an industrial area of Calgary. An old friend of mine, Dan Mackay, "rented" the space to me for free. I worked day and night trying to get the business up and running as well as hustling for clients. Later, I signed a lease to move downtown to be closer to my clients. The lease was more than I could afford, and for three nerve-racking months we lost money while I ran around each day frantically digging up new clients and new business. I hired my first recruiter in 1995 at a salary of CA$40,000, which was very generous at the time (it was also forty thousand times more than what I was earning). It put me back in negative cash flow, but I believed it was a risk worth taking. And before too long, the gamble paid off: we were in the black. Briefly. Trust me, one of the hardest commitments is sticking with long-term goals and objectives when everyone else is focused on the short term.

I worked 120 hours a week when we started the company. Every weekday, after I had finished making all the calls to potential clients and handling all the sales meetings in my regular day job, I would do eight hours of billable programming. I worked weekends, I worked evenings, I didn't know what else to do but work. For years, we paid ourselves the minimum to survive and put the majority of the business income into supporting the growing payroll in the company. My wife gave me an allowance each day, enough for a Diet Coke and Sausage McMuffin on my drive in. At the time, it was a royal treat.

I believed in myself, which was fortunate, because for a long time hardly anyone else did. I remember early on my father surprised me by asking me out for coffee and a doughnut. All he wanted to know was when I planned to throw in the towel. He wasn't the only one. After about three months on the job, one recruiter I hired came into my office with a question: "How are you going to keep the doors open?" I admitted that we were losing money at the time but that I was confident we were about to turn things around. She didn't seem convinced.

Twice in the first ten years the banks pulled out on me overnight. One day the TD Bank called me with a startling update: "Sorry, we're pulling out." It didn't matter to them that we'd always made payments on time and always operated within our covenants. Another company similar to mine had gone bankrupt, and the bank had contracted a case of cold feet. The other time, my account manager at CIBC, with whom I believed I had a solid relationship, called me in and asked if I "really thought IT consulting was going to last." Of course I said "Absolutely," which was obviously the wrong answer because I was bluntly informed that I had ninety days to find a new bank.

We funded the start-up of S.i. Systems and lived off the credit line my wife got from the bank, using our credit cards for cash advances to pay rent and buy groceries. One day I had to tell my wife that even with the line of credit and credit cards, it wasn't enough. We had to sell the house we had leased out and invest the equity to meet payroll and to provide additional cash for us to live on while we worked toward profitability. After all we had been through, the idea of losing our house was devastating. We were crushed. She asked me what the other choice was. "Close the business down," I said. She thought for a moment.

"We'll sell the house."

Trust me, that depth of belief is rare and worth millions.

After 1996 or so, we started to see the needle pointing in the right direction. I was able to pay myself a salary (a depressingly small salary, but it was a start!). We muddled through and worked as hard as we could, but we were just breaking even. I needed help. Luckily, I found it. His name was Doug Bouey. Doug chaired a business group that I joined in 1994 and remained a member of it for twenty-seven years. (Technically, my company didn't qualify at the time for membership, but Doug must have taken pity on me. He let me slide in under the radar.) It was through Doug's and the group's mentorship that I became familiar with some core business concepts. We made some big moves over the next decade.

By 2006, the company was doing CA$50 million in revenue and turning a reasonable profit. We decided to take a quantum jump in terms of scale. Doug recommended that we take advantage of the amazing economic growth at the time, and we boldly challenged our managers to double our revenue in one year to $100 million. Everyone thought we were nuts! Do in one year what it had taken us eleven years? It was insanity! But it was exciting, too. There is an exhilarating energy in the prospect of achieving the impossible. The mood at the meeting was electric. Discussing scenarios felt like we were launching a major military operation. The planning stage was complete by the end of June, and it was time to roll out the campaign.

The first creeping doubt in my resolve began like an itch. By mid-August, I was still restlessly waiting for that first positive indicator that our plan was working. I was getting cold feet. My business partner, Larry Fichtner, was chairman of the board in our partnership, and I went into his office to suggest we call off the goal to double.

"Larry, do you have a minute to talk about one hundred million in one year?"

"Yes, absolutely," he said. "It's a great goal. It's easy to remember; everyone is still talking about it. What's up?"

"I just wanted to see if you still felt good about it."

"Yes, absolutely."

I nodded. "Thanks, just checking."

"Great," he said. "We are going to make it." It was the right affirmation at the right time from the right person. I left his office with no doubt whatsoever. We had a great strategy, we had great and incredibly talented people, and we believed in our goal. More importantly, I believed in our goal.

As it turned out, Doug was wrong. We didn't make it to $100 million in twelve months. It only took nine. And it couldn't have happened without the incredible talent of mentors like Doug and Larry and the many extraordinary colleagues I was lucky enough to work with over the years.

One of the most valuable skills any business leader can have is a nose for good people. Looking back at our humble beginnings, I realize I have been very lucky in that respect. We managed to attract some of the savviest and most hard-working and dedicated professionals in the business. Like adolescence, however, every growth spurt created some discomfort. New challenges require new skill sets, and not everyone has those skill sets. Tough and regrettable decisions, including layoffs, had to be made.

Growth is not the only determinant of success; success also requires an understanding of complexity and the ability to see new solutions to problems when they are not obvious or easy. Our mission is to provide professionals for contract assignments across Canada in the field of information technology (IT). The world, however, isn't standing still, and neither can we. We are constantly changing and upgrading. In 2020, we developed a talent pool of cyber security specialists for our clients to draw from. These IT pros have to constantly upgrade their skills as programming languages change, data analytics explode from social media, functions move onto the phone from the desktop, networks move into the cloud, and secure endpoints extend into the home.

And they did it. We were honoured to be recognized by the Canada's Best Managed Companies awards program, requalifying as a Platinum Club member in 2017, 2018, and 2019, when sale of the business moved majority ownership outside of Canada and prevented us from applying. What makes me proud is having had a hand in creating an environment where many talented individuals from all walks of life and backgrounds found their opportunity to flourish and thrive. Each in his and her own way are wealth creators. After all, wealth doesn't create itself; neither do governments, although politicians generally are only too happy to go into debt to comply (as perilously mounting federal and provincial debt figures attest).

In a society built on the idea that individual flourishing is a benefit to all, my concern is that blanket criticism of the one percent as "bad for society" will marginalize and disincentivize future creators of wealth. In essence, it could turn off the taps of wealth creation. We want to be expanding the one percent, not threatening it with extinction. The one thing we can be certain about is that we cannot merely redistribute our way to prosperity. Punishing prosperity is a failed message.

We need wealth creators. A vibrant economy cannot be imposed from the top down. We need talented, hard-working individuals with big dreams and big ambitions.

Otherwise, it will be up to the prosperity fairies.

CHAPTER 2

THE GAP BETWEEN RICH AND POOR

In fall 2019, freshly minted Canadian NDP leader Jagmeet Singh and his party had not done well in the federal election. Celebrations at NDP headquarters in Burnaby, BC, were sagging at half-mast. The crowd was doing its best to manufacture a positive vibe, but disappointment lay heavy in the air. Singh was making his concession speech after an unexpectedly bruising defeat.

Singh put on a brave smile. The battle had been lost, he said, but not the war! In front of the enthusiastic and boisterous home crowd, he talked about working constructively with the opposition and being a positive force for change, including prioritizing the fight against climate change, affordable housing, capped cellphone rates, pharmacare costs, free college education for all, reconciliation with our Indigenous population, racial and gender justice, and so on. It was time to wrap it up. But not before a soaring send-off. A final call to arms. No defeat. No surrender.

"We're going to make sure that the super wealthy start paying their fair share!"

The crowd roared its approval and erupted into a chant that rolled through the room like a storm.

"Tax the rich! Tax the rich!" Singh grinned, clearly enjoying the chant. "We're on it!" he promised. He threw a clenched fist into the air. He insisted to anyone who would listen that the party's "super wealth tax" was a top priority for supporting a minority government.

"Tax … the … rich! Tax … the … rich! … TAX … THE … RICH!"

Yes, the NDP lost big time in that election. The party won only 16 percent of the vote, and twenty-four seats in Parliament. Yet their chant echoed the complaints we've been hearing all over North America about the very rich and their apparent excesses and misdeeds. It would be a mistake to dismiss these protests. While they're not about to overturn capitalism, these critics of the rich are building a narrative in the public mind that the one-percenters are bad for society. Yet they ignore the fact that without the one-percenters, life will be far less prosperous for everyone, socialists included.

How Complaints about One-Percenters Started

Complaints about capitalism are as old as the capitalist system itself, but the latest wave began in 2008, when global financial markets were rocked to their foundations by the worst financial crisis since the Great Depression. The US government under Republican president George W. Bush and incoming Democratic president Barack Obama rushed to the rescue to prevent another Great Depression. They saved the economic system by investing in the very financiers who caused the problem in the first place.

What is not reported is how it all turned out. What happened to the tremendous amount of money the US government and the average taxpayer paid toward the bailout of the financial system? The ProPublica bailout tracker follows where taxpayer money went. Altogether, accounting for both the Troubled Asset Relief Program (TARP) and the Fannie Mae and Freddie Mac bailout, the government spent US$635 billion. Since then, $390 billion of principal has been repaid, and the US Treasury has collected $353 billion in revenue from its investments. In other words, the government has made a profit. As of August 30, 2021, ProPublica reports, the US government and the average American taxpayer realized a significant net profit on the bailouts. So the bailout was not a gift, but an investment that is being paid back.

Yet that part of the story doesn't get much press. Instead, people are angry about the government money flowing to rich people. Anti-capitalist protests featuring calls to "tax the rich" and "arrest the 1%" popped up in cities all over North America and Europe. During this time, President Obama could have eased the grassroots outrage by telling the public why it was essential to put the institutions that created the crisis back in business—but he chose not to.

A couple of years later, in 2011, the backlash spawned the Occupy movement, which took as its motto "We are the 99 percent!" Social justice advocates targeted what they considered extortionist levels of wealth and concentration of wealth in the hands of a tiny few, the one percent. Originating on Wall Street in New York, the Occupy movement swept around the world, including Canadian cities like Vancouver, Toronto, and Calgary. (By the way, there's no consistent definition of the one percent; it varies as is convenient when hunting the rich.)

A compelling view of the grassroots movement was put forward by French economist Thomas Piketty with the publication of his international bestseller *Capital in the Twenty-First Century.*

He shone the light on wealth "as a major source of economic inequality." Here's what he said in the book:

> For millions of people, "wealth" amounts to little more than a few weeks' wages in a checking account or low-interest savings account, a car, and a few pieces of furniture. The inescapable reality is this: wealth is so concentrated that a large segment of society is virtually unaware of its existence, so that some people imagine that it belongs to surreal or mysterious entities. That is why it is so essential to study capital and its distribution in a methodical, systematic way.

The book sold more than 1.5 million copies worldwide. Piketty argues that when the rate of return on capital is greater than the rate of economic growth over the long term, the result is concentration of wealth. This unequal distribution of wealth causes social and economic instability. "The right solution is a progressive annual tax on capital," Piketty argues in his book. He's calling for a progressive annual global wealth tax of up to 2 percent, combined with a progressive income tax rate reaching as high as 80 percent. He goes on to say: "This will make it possible to avoid an endless inegalitarian spiral while preserving competition and incentives for new instances of primitive accumulation."

It amounts to a war on the rich, and Piketty's proposed wealth tax comes with some very real economic consequences. History has shown time and again that money is fluid, and when taxes get too high or the economic environment becomes otherwise unfavourable, the wealthy move, and the benefits to the countries they live in go with them.

Back to Piketty. His opus was enthusiastically embraced by politicians, academics, media pundits, and social justice advocates. He tapped into what seemed to be increasingly widespread grievances among many that the wealthy were taking advantage of the system. It's become a rallying cry of the left. Democratic presidential candidates Elizabeth Warren and Bernie Sanders (both huge Piketty fans) proposed wealth taxes in the US presidential contests in 2016 and 2020. The idea of making the rich pay more for social programs also helped to catapult Democratic candidate Alexandria Ocasio-Cortez to victory in New York's 14th congressional district race in 2018.

This influential book, and the events that preceded its publication, backed up a new and powerful story in the media, and in the hearts and minds of individuals. The story is a simple one: it's the rich versus the poor. Rich people are helping themselves to most of the world's wealth. They're committing crimes or paying off politicians to stay rich. They're twisting the system for their own benefit.

CEO COMPENSATION

The above argument was bolstered by the widening income gap between CEOs and the people who work for them. In 1964, the ratio of a chief executive's pay to a worker's was 20:1; by 2017, it was 312:1. According to the Economic Policy Institute, a think tank that researches the impact of economic trends and policies on working people in the United States, CEO compensation has jumped 940 percent since 1978 while typical worker compensation has gone up only 12 percent in that same time. Yet critics of the inflated CEO pay overlook one key fact: the explosion in CEO compensation was created by government rules meant to control executive pay packages. Legislation introduced by President Bill Clinton in 1993 set a cap of US$1 million on the tax deductibility of executive compensation. But then, as Sarah Anderson described in an article in *The Agenda*, politics undermined the whole plan:

> After their election victory, Clinton's top economic advisers persuaded the president (over Labor Secretary Robert Reich's objections) to insert a huge loophole in his Proposal. So-called "performance" pay, including stock options and certain bonuses, would be exempted from the deductibility cap. Congress passed this proposal as part of a larger tax bill in 1993. In response, companies began limiting salaries to around $1 million and defining the vast bulk of compensation as a reward for "performance."

This move enriched the CEO who increased the value of the shares. To be sure, everyone benefited—pension funds, retirees, governments, all stockholders—and so did the CEO. This dramatically inflated executive pay packages, and pretty soon, companies were hiking CEO bonuses even more to attract the best talent. In the top 350 firms in the United States, the average CEO pay, including stock options, is a staggering US$17.2 million. If you don't like that, remember that the majority of shares are owned by individuals— and when the value of their stockholdings go up, it's a win for everyone.

POLITICIANS ARE LISTENING

Reports about the big gap between rich and poor are starting to influence the politicians at the most senior level. Canadian prime minister Justin Trudeau, for instance, recently wrote an editorial in which he claimed that "unlike times before, virtually all of the benefits of [economic] growth has accrued to a small number of wealthy Canadians." Even those who believe in the capitalist system are starting to listen to these complaints. Perceived inequality and excessive wealth can fuel anger that the system is rigged, that it's corrupt. This can have a profound impact. It can destabilize a democracy, make people lose faith in the system because it's supposedly rigged. In that environment, the strongman looks like an appealing alternative to a system rigged against honest, poor people. Hence the emergence of "anti-corruption" strongmen around the world, in countries like Turkey and Brazil. Ironically, strongmen who step in to wipe out corruption somehow become billionaires themselves, even while their population suffers.

Yet for all the headlines about wealth inequality, a closer look at the issue reveals a more nuanced picture. Several studies, for instance, criticize Piketty's methods and question whether the gap between rich and poor is as big as advertised. One of the studies comes from economists Chris Edwards and Ryan Bourne of the Cato Institute. They looked at a widely reported study claiming that from 1980 to 2014 the top one percent wealth share jumped more than 16 percentage points. In fact, a careful review of the same data by a group of researchers concluded that the rise had been closer to 6 points.

"The top 1 percent wealth share has risen in recent years," Edwards and Bourne say, "but the change has not been large over the past half century given the large structural changes in the US economy." They further explained that data on wealth inequality often "leaves out human capital and social programs such as Social Security, which has exaggerated estimates of inequality." Omissions of this kind can lead to cases of casual but misleading equivalence, like assuming a wealth gap in Canada is the same as in Iran. Numbers on their own without context can lead to nonsensical conclusions.

THE WAR ON POVERTY

With all the complaints about the growing gap
between rich and poor, you might ask yourself: How
does this affect the lives of people at the bottom of the
ladder? Are the poor worse off—or better off—when
some people get richer? Does the gap have any impact
on the real issues the poor face—getting a job, improving health, finding a stable home, or getting the kids
into college?

If we agree that the real issue is lifting people
out of poverty, the perceived conflict between the
one percent and everyone else is one big distraction.
It's a politically popular distraction too. It's much easier to complain about people who are rich than it is
to bring in long-term policies that actually do something
to help families in need. So the rich become a target
for those virtue signalling that they want to improve
the lives of the poor. It wasn't always that way, though.

Back in January 1964, only a few months after the
assassination of President John F. Kennedy, President
Lyndon Johnson declared war on poverty. His inaugu-
ral address is worth quoting at some length:

Unfortunately, many Americans live on the outskirts of hope—some because of their poverty, and some because of their color, and all too many because of both. Our task is to help replace their despair with opportunity. This administration today, here and now, declares unconditional war on poverty in America.

I urge this Congress and all Americans to join with me in that effort.

It will not be a short or easy struggle, no single weapon or strategy will suffice, but we shall not rest until that war is won. The richest nation on earth can afford to win it. We cannot afford to lose it ... Poverty is a national problem, requiring improved national organization and support. But this attack, to be effective, must also be organized at the state and the local level and must be supported and directed by state and local efforts.

For the war against poverty will not be won here in Washington. It must be won in the field, in every private home, in every public office, from the courthouse to the White House.

"We shall not rest until that war is won," promised the new president. "The richest nation on earth can afford to win it. We cannot afford to lose it." I think it is significant that the president talked about the

United States as a rich nation, not a nation with a small elite of extremely rich individuals. Even in declaring war on poverty, America, in his words, was proudly the "richest nation on earth." Its wealth was not a source of weakness or something to be discouraged or demonized (or confiscated), but its greatest strength and asset. His call was not us against them, but us for and in aid of them. Poverty was a national problem that required a national solution.

Fast-forward to today.

What's happened to people on the lowest economic rung of society since LBJ declared his war on poverty?

First, we have to understand that the recent COVID-19 pandemic can easily colour our perceptions. Government-enforced lockdowns caused a spike in poverty as businesses that typically employ low-income workers, like restaurants, hotels, and other service industries, shut their doors. Low-wage workers suffered job losses three times worse than during the 2008–09 recession and at nearly seven times the rate of high-income earners. The crisis also unduly affected women, since the closure of schools and daycares saw them bear most of the burden of staying home with the kids and even taking on homeschooling. A year after the lockdowns began, ten times more women than men had fallen out of the labour force, setting back much of the progress women had made in the job market in recent decades.

But step back from this extreme outlier of a year and look at the long-term picture, and you'll see it's far more optimistic.

In the decades since Johnson launched the war on poverty in 1964, poverty rates in the United States have declined dramatically. While economists have come up with different numbers to portray the decline, one recent statistic from a division of the Federal Reserve is particularly striking. To create a more accurate comparison between poverty in 1963 and in recent years, Federal Reserve economists developed the "full income poverty measure," including cash income, taxes, and major in-kind transfers and updated poverty thresholds for inflation annually. Using this measure, the full income poverty rate based on Johnson's standards fell from 19.5 percent to 2.3 percent by 2017.

This tremendous achievement in poverty reduction is far from an America-only phenomenon. Canada monitors the "low income cut-off," or LICO, which refers to the threshold below which a family will spend more of its after-tax income on food, shelter, and clothing than the average family. In 1976, 13 percent of Canadians were living below this threshold. By 2014, it had fallen to 8.8 percent.

Meanwhile, across the world, poverty has been in retreat over the past thirty years, as David R. Henderson, a research fellow with the Hoover Institution, observed in a 2018 article:

> For the first time in world history, fewer than one billion people in the world live in extreme poverty. This is all the more striking when you remember that the world population, at 7.6 billion people, is at an all-time high. Why has this happened? Because of increased international trade and economic growth—which have made some people extremely wealthy, while also lifting over one billion others out of crippling destitution. The argument that economic inequality somehow exacerbates poverty is specious.

WHY WE'RE WINNING THE WAR ON POVERTY

This reduction in global poverty is an extraordinary achievement—for the free enterprise system. It's a simple fact that as the world has grown more open and interconnected through the trade of goods, services, and ideas, and as individual freedom and open competition has taken root across the globe, those on the bottom rung of the economic ladder have been lifted up. The last quarter century has seen steady progress toward these principles during a time that corresponded with global GDP more than doubling. One way to measure the march of the free enterprise system is the Index of Economic Freedom, an annual ranking by the Heritage Foundation that analyzes the economic policies of 184 countries and ranks them based on four pillars of economic freedom: rule of law, government size, regulatory efficiency, and open markets. The average score has risen from 57.1 in the mid-1990s to 61.6 in 2021—though it should be noted that in both Canada and the United States, the economic freedom index has slumped lower over the past decade during a time when both countries saw an increase in regulatory and tax burdens. Since 2011, the States' ranking on the list has fallen from 9th to 20th while Canada's has gone from 6th place to 9th, less dramatic but still troubling. But not surprising, since tax burdens are an important component of the index and the total tax bill of the average Canadian family over the last decade grew at the fastest pace since the 1980s, as figures from the Fraser Institute's Canadian Consumer Tax Index show. Households now spend about 43 percent of their income on taxes, outpacing the 36 percent they spend on the basic necessities of life like shelter, food, and clothing.

At an individual level, the free market has given people like me the opportunity to create new companies and live (or die) by the laws of supply and demand. Competition can be brutal. In our system you might win, but you can just as easily be crushed. The companies that survive create jobs and make everyone wealthier. Yes, the biggest successes make their founders and top executives rich, but that's the inevitable and (in my opinion) welcome result of building companies, jobs, and communities.

Need more evidence that the free enterprise system works best? You need only look at countries that have eschewed open economies and embraced autocratic socialism. Consider the sad case of Argentina, one of the world's perennial economic basket cases of the modern era, known for its frequent debt defaults. It wasn't always that way, though. From 1870 until the early 1930s, Canada and Argentina followed a similar path in terms of their per capita growth rates, but in response to the Great Depression, the Latin American nation pursued a self-destructive system of income redistribution, rejection of foreign investment, and implementation of trade and price controls. The result: from 1935 to 2018, Argentina managed to grow its per capita GDP by less than half the rate seen in Canada, translating into squandered opportunities and reduced living standards for its citizens.

An even starker example can be seen in Venezuela, where Hugo Chávez embarked on a grand agenda starting in 2000 of nationalizing industries, massively increasing government spending, and enforcing price controls that crippled the country's private sector, all under the mantle of "21st century socialism." While incomes and employment soared, it was only a temporary boost courtesy of the nation's vast oil reserves; once petroleum prices collapsed, so too did Venezeula's veneer of prosperity. Gripped by a hyperinflation crisis in which, as the *Wall Street Journal* observed, a schoolteacher must earn a month's salary to buy a dozen eggs and two pounds of cheese, the country has wiped out half a century of economic growth.

IT'S NOT A ZERO-SUM GAME

There's no question that the free enterprise system has lifted millions of people worldwide out of poverty. Yet it's suffering a crisis of confidence among younger adults. A 2019 survey by Gallup found that among Millennials (born 1981 to 1996) and Gen Zers (born

1997 to 2012), socialism is now as popular as capitalism. Whereas a decade ago, 66 percent of people in those demographics held a positive view of capitalism, that view fell to just 51 percent by 2019, with socialism seen in a positive light by 49 percent.

This is only emboldening left-wing critics who are, as we will see, increasingly calling on governments to impose huge taxes on the rich to pay for services to the poor to enable them to climb out of poverty. That's a mistake. It has not worked in the past, and it won't work today. It's wrong thinking to focus on the gap between rich and poor because the real issue should be the condition of people at the bottom of the ladder. "If the problem we care about is poverty, then the calls to tax the rich and reduce income inequality are misguided," says David Henderson of the Hoover Institution. "Instead, we should be cheering for policies that lead to higher economic growth."

Ryan Messmore, a research fellow at the Heritage Foundation, agrees. Evidence of a widening gap is "troubling," he writes, but "implicit in much of the critique of our income divide is the assumption that inequality per se is inherently unjust, and therefore the gap between the rich and the poor is as well." Efforts directed at eradicating poverty "are frequently derailed by misguided ideology—in particular, by the notion that poverty is best understood through the lens of inequality. Far too often, policy makers succumb to the argument that a widening gap between the richest and poorest ... is the fundamental problem to be solved and that poverty is merely a symptom of that deepest flaw."

Is the gap really a problem? In other words, does the very presence of billionaires mean that poor people are worse off? Are the rich taking from the poor?

The erroneous idea that the economy is like a pie that's fixed in size is at the heart of such thinking. If that were the case, then yes, the more billionaires you have, the less pie there is for everyone else to divvy up among themselves. But that's not how the economy works. The pie isn't fixed in size. It grows when people invest, take risks, innovate, and transform their ideas into businesses that employ other people and provide them, in turn, with the means and wealth to spend and invest and improve their lives. That's how economies grow, how pies get bigger. For people to apply their skills and take those risks, however, there needs to be a motivating reward. So some people get a larger slice of that expanding pie—but the smaller slices increase in size too. It's why a poor person in Canada today is better off than someone who was poor twenty-five, fifty, or one hundred years ago, even if the richer have gotten richer. At the bottom level, not only income but also the standard of living has risen over time.

Of course, if you want to see the starkest example of a growing pie in action, consider China. The number of billionaires has exploded since the 1990s from virtually none to more than 1,000 in 2020, according to the Hurun Global Rich List. Over the last forty years, as China embraced market reforms, some 800 million people were lifted out of poverty.

CHAPTER 3

WHO ARE THE RICH, ANYWAY?

In January 2020, TVO's Steve Paikin hosted a debate on his show, *The Agenda*. It posed the question "Should billionaires be taxed out of existence?" The debate, which captured the zeitgeist of the times, gave the Yes side plenty of airtime: "Billionaires are not only rich, they are incomprehensibly rich," said Linda McQuaig, author of several books, including *The Trouble with Billionaires: Why Too Much Money at the Top Is Bad for Everyone*. She went on to say that the vast fortunes of billionaires

were often acquired due to political connections ... or simply from inheritance, you know, the lucky circumstances of birth, or what Warren Buffett calls the ovarian lottery ... People should be rewarded for hard work ... but today's rewards at the top are, quite frankly, absurd and completely out of line. Take the richest person in Canada, David Thomson. He saw his fortune grow in the last five years from 20 billion dollars to 40 billion dollars. That's four billion dollars a year. So that means that his income in those years was 80,000 times the income of the ordinary Canadian worker, like a nurse. Did [David Thomson] work 80,000 times as hard as the typical nurse? Was his contribution worth 80,000 times what a nurse's is?

What Linda McQuaig got wrong was that David Thomson wasn't earning $4 billion a year: his assets were. This would be like a farmer whose asset, his land, rises in value or a homeowner whose asset, a house, rises in value. The farmer and homeowner aren't earning more money or having more money to spend; their asset is increasing in value. At the same time as David Thomson's assets, acquired by three generations of hard work and risk takers starting with his grandfather, rose in value, so too did pension funds, government treasuries, and the general stock market. David Thomson's assets didn't increase their value in a vacuum; many other Canadians benefitted from the same bump.

THE ONE-PERCENTERS

It's fashionable these days to complain about the rich. Yet when critics rant against wealthy people, they don't tell you who they are and how they accumulated that wealth. When you do look at the so-called one-percenters, you might be surprised: the rich are not who you might think.

In 1984, fewer than half the people on the Forbes 400 list of richest Americans were self-made. Most of the people on that Forbes 400 list inherited their wealth. In stark contrast, by 2018, the self-made comprised 67 percent of the list. In other words, two-thirds of the richest people in America made their money from scratch in their lifetime. What about in Canada? According to a poll conducted by BMO, two-thirds of Canada's millionaires are self-made. The poll looked at Canadians with more than $1 million in investible wealth: almost half were either immigrants or first-generation Canadians, and nearly seven out of ten made their money on Canadian soil. In doing so, they created a lot of prosperity around them. "Today's high-net worth Canadians, whether they were born here or have adopted Canada as their own, prove that hard work and an entrepreneurial spirit can result in prosperity and success," said Alex Dousmanis-Curtis, senior vice-president and head of BMO Harris Private Banking, in a BMO press release.

Think about that. What a great result for Canada's pro-immigration policies. They've delivered some fantastic entrepreneurs who have made us all richer.

Tobias Lütke, for instance, came to Canada from Germany in 2002, a twenty-two-year-old high-school dropout who, rather than go to university, took a job as an apprentice in computer programming at a subsidiary of Siemens, the multinational industrial manufacturer. Now worth about US$10 billion (as of 2021) and counting, he is the co-founder and CEO of Shopify, the multinational, Ottawa-based e-commerce platform he built from a snowboarding website. In early 2021, the company was ranked the most valuable organization in Canada. Lütke now focuses on environmental philanthropy, complete with a $5-million annual sustainability fund.

Gina Parvaneh Cody emigrated from Iran in 1979 to pursue a graduate degree in engineering. She came to Canada with only $2,000. She would become a pathbreaker: the first woman in Concordia University's history to complete a PhD in building (structural) engineering. On September 24, 2018, after a successful career at a Woodbridge, Ontario-based engineering company now known as CCI Group, she made history yet again: she donated CA$15 million to her alma mater. Much of it funds several annual scholarships; $250,000 has been earmarked to increase the presence of women and minorities in the historically male faculty.

At the gift announcement ceremony, Cody had a message for all the young girls around the world who have been told time and again that engineering and computers are for boys only. "Hear me now," she said. "My name is Gina Cody and I am a woman and I am an engineer. This is my school and I say engineering and computer science is for everyone, regardless of gender, ethnicity or wealth."

The fact that so many immigrants have come to Canada to put down roots and to create prosperity for themselves, for their families, and for their employees and community is something we should encourage, not discourage. We need more entrepreneurship, not less.

This picture of the new rich in Canada is truly heartening to an entrepreneur like me who believes in equality of opportunity. Technology, free trade, and accessible education are providing equal opportunity as never before in history. And that new group of rich Canadians who are jumping at those opportunities should be admired for the hard work they take on to build companies, and the jobs and prosperity they create for other Canadians.

Take Chip Wilson. The University of Calgary graduate had been successful on the west coast with athletic gear focused on the surfing and snowboarding crowd. Companies like Nike and Adidas were big names in the athletic gear market when Wilson discovered yoga and realized it was being underserved. He also was savvy enough to realize something else: the overwhelming percentage of his customers were young males. Where were the young women? Wilson's answer was to design a line of athletic wear that aligned seamlessly with the values of the burgeoning yoga community. Lululemon was born. Lululemon employed about 19,000 people in 2020, which was up 20 percent from the year before and 52 percent from 2017. It's numbers like these that should remind us that wealth creation is not about profits that seem to constellate at the very top only for the benefit of the very few, but wealth that is spread across the landscape and shared by many.

THE TRIAL OF THE ENTREPRENEUR

It's worth remembering that having an idea and starting a business is no easy street for the entrepreneur.

In fact, most new businesses fail in the early years. The US Bureau of Labor Statistics says that approximately 20 percent of new businesses fail in their first year, and by the end of the fifth year, roughly 50 percent have collapsed. Only one-third of businesses survive ten years.

Those numbers are sobering, yet society in general derides rather than supports entrepreneurs. The skill and effort to create and sustain an enterprise for the long term are very similar to those required to play and stay in pro sports. Few can achieve sports success like Michael Jordan, just as few can achieve business success like Chip Wilson. Running a business requires skill and grit, and it is far from easy.

It takes extraordinary focus and effort to run a successful business, and most people would not want to do the work. When I started S.i. Systems, I worked 80 to 120 hours a week, every week, and gave up a social life of any kind. Bill Gates, Mark Zuckerberg, Ray Kroc—all were fanatical about their craft and spent time and energy on their business with the same grit a Michael Jordan or Wayne Gretzky spent on their games in basketball and hockey.

The story of the founders of Research In Motion (RIM) is a case in point. When recent engineering graduates Mike Lazaridis and his college pal Doug Fregin founded RIM in 1984, the idea that a company they started would end up as the most valuable in Canada was unthinkable. Well, perhaps not for them—and especially not for Lazaridis, who didn't lack for confidence—but absolutely for anyone looking at their venture from the outside. It was madness. And when they failed to bust out of the gates with a big hit, it only confirmed conventional wisdom. Their first big hit was the DigiSync film reader, which proved very popular with the movie business, earning them an Academy Award for technical achievement. On the other hand, innovative software they developed that ultimately revolutionized the infant pager market failed to generate much interest—except from one extremely prescient recent Harvard graduate named Jim Balsillie. He thought these guys were really onto something and bought into their venture with a $250,000 investment he made by remortgaging his house. That bold bet by Balsillie paid off.

Building on the success RIM had with its interactive pager, the company rolled out its highly secure e-mail service, and then in 2002, its first BlackBerry smartphone, which revolutionized the telecom sector. The device was an instant hit with bankers and tech insiders. Balsillie, ever the master marketer, handed out the phone for free at industry conferences and generated buzz in the media so that it quickly became a must-have tech gadget. By 2007, RIM controlled 30 percent of the US smartphone market and counted nine million paid subscribers to its service. That same year, RIM's share price soared to an all-time high, making it the most valuable publicly traded company in Canada, and giving Lazaridis and Balsillie a net worth of over CA$3 billion each.

Every mountain has two sides, though. Up and down. In the case of RIM, its downfall occurred when the leaders—the same great men who grew the company and made it an astounding success—failed to appreciate the threat posed by an upstart in the market called the iPhone. When Apple launched its touchscreen device in 2007, Lazaridis and Balsillie marvelled at how much technology the company had packed into its phones, but because Apple's focus was the consumer market with an emphasis on downloading music and videos, RIM didn't see it as a threat to its core market of business and government users. "It's OK—we'll be fine," is how Balsillie reacted, according to *Losing the Signal* by Jacquie McNish and Sean Silcoff, a book that detailed the company's rise and fall. They didn't see the threat posed by Apple, and the company's fortunes tanked, taking most of Balsillie and Lazaridis's wealth with it.

Making money is hard work; keeping it is even harder. This is the sobering reality that presses on every rich person 24/7, every day of the year.

I don't know how many of you have ever tried to build a business on your own, but it isn't easy. Not by a long shot. It takes much more than an idea, and more time than you would imagine when looking in from the outside. You need to risk something you cherish—your house, your leisure time, your relationships—in a gamble that you will come out on top after a period of intense work. The setbacks, the pressures, the disappointments, the unexpected and unforeseeable problems and complications, the hours, the expense, the mountains of rising debt, the sacrifices, the toll on family, the relentless uphill struggle, the competition, cyber threats or bankruptcy breathing down your neck, not always knowing who to trust, the lonely and usually late-night moments of crippling doubt—all are part of the deal.

Taking risks can take you to the brink, and during the many nights I lay awake sick to my stomach with worry about problems that I had to deal with, I was on my own. It must be the same for professional athletes who put their bodies, their years of effort, dedication, and sacrifice, on the line each time they play. Business is a lot like that.

The mistake many people make is assuming that once a new business is off the ground it's turbulence-free flying. Not so. The corporate world is littered with the obituaries of companies that once dominated their industries, their future success seemingly assured. Some, like RIM (which later changed its name to BlackBerry), were caught off guard by a rival with a better version of their main product. Like RIM, Finnish telecom giant Nokia's dominance of the mobile phone world seemed at one point unstoppable (readers of a certain age will remember how prevalent and instantly recognizable its trademark ring tone was), but it too saw its hold on that market wiped out by rivals. That's also what happened with one-time Internet giant Yahoo!, which dominated the world of web search until Google ate its lunch. Netscape invented the web browser and was a multi-billion-dollar market capitalization until Microsoft gave browsing away for free. Other companies failed to pivot sufficiently when technology disrupted their sectors. Blockbuster was too slow to respond when Netflix disrupted the video-rental market and was left behind when its customers flocked to streaming video on demand. Big names in photography like Kodak and Polaroid also seemed impossibly entrenched until the rise of digital photography left them shells of their former selves.

Meanwhile, other companies faced assaults on multiple fronts. Big name retailers such as Sears, Kmart, and Toys"R"Us eventually folded when confronted by the double-whammy rise of low-cost revolutionaries like Walmart and online shopping in the form of Amazon. All of this is to say, it doesn't matter how strong your history is, you're always potentially one disruption or shock away from having your business upended.

Case in point: Who among us had any idea that in March 2020 the world would be facing a global pandemic that would shut down the economy and take us into a depression?

With the outbreak of the COVID-19 pandemic in March 2020, S.i. Systems saw new business plummet by 60 percent literally overnight. I had been at the helm of the company for almost thirty years, and I thought I had seen it all. Not even close. A business doesn't experience out-of-the-blue bottom-line setbacks that severe and not wonder if that's it. The end.

I had to make truly hard choices. People had to be laid off. People—colleagues and team members—with rents and mortgages and families. Overnight, we had to make arrangements for our remaining employees to work from home. Our whole business model was modified in two days, and we had to improvise a new one. We had to deal with the pressures of staying afloat during a sudden global lockdown. In addition, while the descent was still occurring, we had to plan, strategize, invest, and implement for the eventual return of "normal."

Entrepreneurs Are Major Employers

All to say, entrepreneurship is really hard, yet the payoff to society in terms of jobs and prosperity is outstanding. Entrepreneurs are, hands down, the biggest wealth generators in the countries they live in. Seven in ten workers in the private sector earn a paycheque from small businesses with fewer than one hundred employees, and when you factor in medium-sized businesses that employee one hundred to five hundred workers, small and medium-sized enterprises account for 90 percent of all jobs. And guess what? All these businesses are run by entrepreneurs. As I noted in the preceding chapter, a lot of these job-creating entrepreneurs are immigrants. In fact, according to Statistics Canada, businesses launched by immigrant entrepreneurs are responsible for more new jobs than those started by native-born entrepreneurs. The 2019 study found "firms owned by immigrants accounted for a disproportionate share of net job creation"—they made up 25 percent of net new private-sector jobs created between 2003 and 2013, while accounting for 17 percent of the firms in the study.

S.i. Systems provides meaningful work to just over 4,000 Canadians and is just one of many information technology staffing companies in Canada. In Ontario alone there are 205 companies like mine that provide work for 24,600 high-end professionals, creating revenue in that province of CA\$3.9 billion per year. That is a big impact from just 205 highly skilled entrepreneurs. In the United States, long a beacon of entrepreneurialism to the world, the numbers are also impressive. Independent businesses with fewer than five hundred employees account for 99.7 percent of all jobs in the country, and in the year prior to the pandemic, every month saw roughly 310 out of every 100,000 adults start their own business, according to the Ewing Marion Kauffman Foundation's indicators of entrepreneurialism. Most new businesses fail, but some take root and a few grow to take care of their communities and become world-beaters.

The history books teem with stories of entrepreneurs who transformed a spark of an idea into vast companies that employ tens of thousands of workers and helped build or grow entire communities around them. It takes time, grit, and lots of hard work. Henry

Ford's first two automotive ventures were failures, but eventually his Ford Motor Company grew to reshape Detroit into an elite American city, bringing wealth to thousands of workers with revolutionary initiatives like the "five dollar day" in 1914, when he doubled the daily salary of workers and laid the foundation of the modern American middle class.

In California and then Florida, Walt Disney's vision for a new generation of theme parks reshaped vast stretches of agricultural and swamp land. When Disney flew over the modest city of Orlando and took in its lush environs and network of planned interstates in November 1963, he saw an opportunity to bring to life his vision of a community of tomorrow. Disney died before he could bring his plan to life, but the Walt Disney World theme park inspired an entertainment industry in the region that, as of 2019, employed 463,000 people, or 41 percent of the region's workforce.

Entrepreneurs have left a lasting legacy on many other cities across North America. As a student at Stanford University, Phil Knight dreamed up an idea of tackling Adidas's dominance of the running shoe market by tapping cheap labour in Japan to manufacture lower-cost, higher-quality shoes. After graduating, he teamed up with his track coach in 1964 and, selling sneakers out of the trunk of a car in Portland,

Oregon, launched what would eventually become Nike. As of 2019, Nike's headquarters in the nearby city of Beaverton employed 12,000 people, up from 6,000 in 2006, making it the city's largest employer, according to the loveMONEY website. Just before going public in 1986, Microsoft moved its headquarters to Redmond, Washington; that location employs 53,000 of its worldwide workforce of 166,000. Down the coast, of course, Silicon Valley has been shaped and reshaped over the decades by companies like Fairchild, Intel, Hewlett Packard, Apple, Google, and Facebook that, combined, employ more than 100,000 people in that region alone.

After Walmart, Amazon is the United States' largest employer, with over a million workers as of 2020. Amazon creates meaningful jobs across the spectrum, and they house much of society's critical computer infrastructure. I can't help noticing that in the mainstream media and in trendy political and academic circles, Jeff Bezos is about as popular as mouldy bread. As of this writing, he's worth over US$180 billion, and former US labor secretary Robert Reich has called him a "Scrooge" capitalist. Does this make any sense? Bezos saw business as usual and decided to shake it up. Out of nowhere, and against all the odds, Bezos created a new online store where you could buy and sell books.

It proved to be so successful as a sales channel that it transformed the retail market permanently. A typical month on Amazon's hiring portal lists over fifty thousand new job openings. It's why LinkedIn regularly ranks Amazon as the number-one hirer of new college and university grads each year, providing meaningful entry-level positions to young adults. Aside from the many high-paying technology, finance, and marketing jobs at Amazon, the company also provides employment to vast numbers of low-skilled workers. And contrary to the media-spun myth that these jobs exploit workers with low pay, Amazon's minimum wage of US$15 is double the federal minimum wage. In his 2020 letter to shareholders, Bezos was rightly proud to point out that the lowest-paid Amazon worker earns more than forty million American workers. These workers are paying taxes, investing in their communities, and on a path to financial security because an entrepreneur had a single revolutionary idea. We don't need fewer people like Bezos; we need more.

Consider, as well, the opportunities spawned by these great entrepreneurial innovators. Uber, the brainchild of two already successful founders of tech start-ups, Travis Kalanick and Garrett Camp (who was born in my hometown of Calgary), have revolutionized the ride-sharing market and given nearly four million drivers around the world an opportunity to be their own boss. Shopify has made a wildly lucrative business out of enabling other entrepreneurs by giving them the power to easily set up their own online stores. Boosted by pandemic lockdowns that robbed so many people of their day jobs, Shopify now boasts 1.7 million online merchants, who account for 9 percent of all e-commerce sales in the US. As the company likes to point out, every twenty-eight seconds a new entrepreneur somewhere completes their first sale on Shopify. That is how wealth begets wealth, and it's something we should all be cheering for.

{ CHAPTER 4 }

THE WEALTHY PAY MORE THAN THEIR FAIR SHARE

⊂⊙⊙⊂

Canada's Parliamentary Budget Officer recently reported that the top 1 percent of families in Canada own more than 25 percent of the nation's wealth, while the bottom 40 percent share just over 1 percent. According to media reports, Canada's eighty-seven richest families own as much wealth as three provinces (Newfoundland and Labrador, New Brunswick, and Prince Edward Island) combined. According to an Oxfam report, two Canadian billionaires, David Thomson and the late Galen Weston Sr., are as wealthy as the poorest 30 percent of the country combined.

In 2018, the Canadian Centre for Policy Alternatives (CCPA) issued a report titled *Born to Win: Wealth Concentration in Canada since 1999*. It was a blistering attack on the rich. "Canada's dynastic families have got it all—more wealth, more inheritance, and are as lightly taxed as they were the last time we looked in 2014," said study author and CCPA senior economist David Macdonald. "You'd expect Canada's tax regime would try to counteract this concentration of wealth at the very top, where it's needed the least, but in fact, federal policies encourage it."

Among other things, the CCPA study found that Canada's eighty-seven richest families saw their net worth grow by an average of 37 percent between 2012 and 2016, while middle-income Canadian families saw their net worth grow by only 16 percent over the same period.

What's more, the concentration of wealth has a negative impact on the life of people who are poor, according to Frank Elgar, associate professor at McGill University, Canada Research Chair in Social Inequalities in Child Health. "Food banks are overwhelmed ... Meanwhile, income inequality continues to rise, real wages for half the workforce are stagnant or falling, consumer debt is soaring, and the top 10 percent takes nearly half of all income."

The solution? Pretty predictable: Tax the rich!

That's a perennially popular view. Some 69 percent of Canadians believe the government should increase taxes on wealthy people "in order to support the poor."

Justin Trudeau and his Liberals have vowed to get tough on wealthy people. In the federal government's 2021 budget, they proposed a 10 percent tax on luxury items (cars, boats, private aircraft, and so on) in excess of $100,000. They insisted that the luxury tax would go a long way to help address issues of tax "fairness" by asking the wealthy to "pay a bit more." The tax is projected to generate CA$604 million over five years. It's worth mentioning that former president George H.W. Bush introduced a similar wealth tax. It was repealed by President Bill Clinton. Why? With the tax came fewer purchases and less commerce in the luxury goods market. The tax revenue was minor compared to the massive economic cost of job loss and companies associated with making luxury goods in the United States downsizing, shutting down, and laying off workers.

The NDP wants to go further in a hunt after the rich. The party wants to impose a 1 percent tax on the net worth of those with wealth of over CA$10 million. "The amassing of wealth by the top 1 percent of this country is at an extreme level," said NDP critic for the Treasury Board Matthew Green. "It's absolutely clear, the rich are not paying their fair share. We will never achieve justice and equality if we allow this to continue."

DOES A WEALTH TAX WORK?

Let's look at the concept of a wealth tax. A wealth tax differs from an income tax in that it includes taxing assets already purchased with after-tax dollars. That includes stocks and bonds, paintings, cars, boats, real estate, and jewellery. It is in essence a second tax on items you already paid for with money you earned and already paid taxes on.

The wealth tax is a very old idea, as old as money itself. We know of wealth taxes in ancient Greece around 500 BCE. During crises, like a war, for instance, it was common for wealthy Greeks to be taxed to pay for the mercenaries needed to keep Athens safe for democracy. In like manner, medieval kings often made a nuisance of themselves dunning lords in their domain for new cash to top up the treasury. France had a wealth tax from 1982 to 1986 and again from 1988 to 2017. The top rate was between 1.5 percent and 1.8 percent, with the total tax rate on fortunes larger than 13 million euros (US$14.3 million at the time of writing) hovering at about 1.4 percent. By 1990, a dozen European countries had imposed a wealth tax on its wealthiest citizens.

So what happened? How did the wealth tax work out for the countries that implemented it? For the vast number of European countries with a new wealth tax, it was an epic flop. German courts declared the government's wealth tax unconstitutional "because of its confiscatory nature." France's president, Emmanuel Macron, killed that country's wealth tax in 2018 after it triggered an epic migration of its richest people out of the country. Worse for France, the wealth tax didn't do what the tax-grab crowd thought it would. According to French economist Eric Pinchet, it cost the government more than US$125 billion in capital flight from 1998 to 2006, yet only generated about $26 billion in revenue for government coffers. "It's all well and good to want to spread wealth," Macron told reporters as he cancelled the tax, "but you first need to produce, to create wealth before redistributing, that's how it works."

Why does a wealth tax fail? It chases the entrepreneurial class, who create the wealth in the first place, out of the country.

Additionally, a wealth tax "can be really difficult
to administer and ensure even a moderate compliance
rate," according to the director of global projects at the
non-partisan Tax Foundation. Evaluating the market
value of even a single asset—a painting, for instance—
is very difficult, requires highly specialized expertise,
and can be monstrously time consuming and expen-
sive. Try to imagine a Canada Revenue Agency tax
expert assessing the fair market value of hundreds
of different assets whose values can change from one
year to the next.

By 2019, only four of the dozen European countries
that brought in wealth taxes still had them. Spain's wealth
tax (ironically) was imposed two years after the death
of the authoritarian leader Francisco Franco and, curi-
ously, exempts residents of Madrid. Norway charges
0.85 percent on wealth above NOK1.48 million,
or CA\$223,000. Belgium introduced a tax on securities
valued at over half a million euros. Switzerland has
a wealth tax of 0.3 percent to 1.0 percent of net worth.
So a small number of countries have had, at best, modest success with a wealth tax, but most have not, and
in none of these countries does the wealth tax consti-
tute a significant source of revenue.

What about Canada? Would a wealth tax bring
in a lot of money? The C.D. Howe Institute says no:

The "benefit of implementing [an annual wealth tax] alongside a capital income tax does not compensate for the significant administrative costs that would be involved," C.D. Howe analysis concluded in 2019. In other words, even if we could tax wealth, we shouldn't—it isn't worth it. Besides, the revenue from a Canadian wealth tax would only cover a week and a half of government spending.

INCOME TAX

We've been talking about a wealth tax on a person's assets. But what about the tax on income, such as earned income from work, or income from investments?

The majority of people in a country believe that rich people do not pay their fair share of income taxes. A federal poll conducted in late summer 2019 by the Canada Revenue Agency reported that only 28 percent of Canadians believe wealthy people are paying their fair share in taxes.

Yet the actual numbers might surprise many.

In a progressive tax system such as Canada's, those at the top are paying the highest rate and the largest amount of taxes of any cohort. And that's as it should be. What isn't talked about at all is how much more

the rich pay than everyone else. For instance, according to the Fraser Institute, the top 10 percent of earners
in Canada pay more than half of all income taxes
collected each year. The top 10 percent of earners,
by the way, include anyone making over CA$96,000
per year, which would include a lot of policemen and
bureaucrats.

The Fraser Institute article, by economist Philip
Cross, uses Statistics Canada figures to make
an important point: over the past four decades, the
share of total taxes from the rich has increased steeply
compared to other groups, from about 44 percent
in 1987 to 54 percent in 2017. "Far from not paying their
fair share," notes Cross, "the top 10 percent of income
earners in Canada have long been the only group that
pays more in total taxes than their share of income."

Someone should tell the Canadian Centre for Policy
Alternatives: the rich are already paying for the rest
of us.

Raising the income tax rate above 50 percent often
ends up reducing total tax revenues. Just after he took
office in 2015, Prime Minister Trudeau hiked the top
federal personal income tax rate from 29 percent
to 33 percent. With provincial taxes, the top rates
in some provinces were now over 50 percent. One
year later, the Parliamentary Budget Officer estimated

that the increase would actually reduce Ottawa's tax revenues.

"It took most governments a long time to admit this," *Globe and Mail* columnist Konrad Yakabuski wrote in the spring of 2021.

> Tax rates soared in the aftermath of the Second World War. But by 1980, when the top US marginal income tax rate stood at 70 per cent, it had become clear that higher tax rates did not always translate into higher revenues.

> Under President Ronald Reagan, Congress cut it first to 50 per cent, and then to 28 per cent. While many economists believe Mr. Reagan went too far, his tax cuts fueled the economic boom of the 1980s and radically changed the way governments thought about tax policy.

The Canadian-born Nobel Prize–winning economist Robert Mundell made the argument that raising taxes on the wealthy produces negative results for government coffers, Yakabuski continued. He quotes Mundell's 1999 interview with the CBC: "'Any tax rate, once it gets above 30 per cent, becomes counterproductive. It inhibits growth and therefore reduces future tax revenues. When a country has higher tax rates than its neighbours, you suffer from brain drain.'"

MONEY MOVES

If you want to see brain drain in action, just look at Europe's various plans to tax their way out of debt over the decades. In the 1960s and '70s, the Labour government in the United Kingdom introduced a number of measures to hike taxes on the rich. In 1974, the top income tax rate was 83 percent, and when an investment income surcharge was added, it hit 98 percent. Very few individuals were actually charged this top rate, but its existence had a deep impact. The government action spurred many of the country's rich—industrialists, bankers, actors, and several high-profile musicians— to flee. David Bowie decamped to Switzerland. Tom Jones fled to Los Angeles. The Rolling Stones moved to France, where they recorded the aptly titled album *Exile on Main St.* while sheltering their wealth in the Netherlands. "We had to leave England to acquire enough money to pay the taxes because in those days, in England, the high tax rate was 90 percent, so that's very hard," lead singer Mick Jagger later said. "You made 100 pounds, they took 90."

In France, where the rich were already subject to punitive wealth taxes, the socialist government of François Hollande announced, in 2012, a 75 percent supertax on incomes of more than 1 million euros. Between the wealth taxes and supertax on high incomes, an estimated 42,000 millionaires moved out of the country in a ten-year stretch from 2002 to 2012. They included France's richest man, Bernard Arnault, CEO of luxury group LVMH, and superstar actor Gérard Depardieu. Hollande was forced to scrap the supertax after just two years and his successor, Macron, who famously quipped that the supertax made the country like "Cuba without the sun," scaled back France's tax on the assets of the wealthy.

It can't be overstated how easily wealthy individuals and their businesses can pull up roots and move to jurisdictions that are more welcoming of their efforts. The effects can be devastating to an economy. Quebec's experience after the 1976 election of the Parti Québécois and the 1980 independence referendum is telling. Until then, Montreal was on par with Toronto as Canada's business capital, but with an unfriendly political climate for business conducted in English, several of the largest companies moved headquarters down the 401 to Toronto, including Royal Bank of Canada, Bank of Montreal, and Sun Life Financial. Tens of thousands of young people also fled the province in a devastating loss of human capital. The city and province have never fully recovered from the long economic malaise that followed.

Despite these examples of how mobile money can be, and how higher taxes drive away the wealth creators, we see governments parading these doomed schemes for votes. In the US, the high-tax state of California has seen hundreds of businesses flee to Texas in the past few years, citing less red tape and more attractive taxes. Elon Musk has moved to Texas and plans to shift Tesla's head office there. The same is true of Hewlett Packard, Oracle, Pabst Brewing Company, and Digital Realty Trust. Now New York, already a high-tax state, is planning on joining New Jersey to hike taxes on those earning more than $1 million, and business leaders are openly being courted by political leaders in Florida about moving their operations there. The loss would potentially cripple New York State's finances—personal income taxes already account for two-thirds of the state's tax revenue, and 40 percent of those personal income taxes are paid by the top 1 percent of income earners.

All this to show, a wealth tax reduces the number of rich people in a country, who are the ones paying the majority of the taxes. It drives away the people who build wealth for others. And it incents our rich people to relocate to jurisdictions where the tax rate is lower. Many of our rich people will—as we have seen in France, Britain, and California—simply leave.

It's happening now. Canadians for Tax Fairness estimates that Canadian corporations have relocated as much as CA$199 billion in offshore accounts in more tax-friendly countries such as Barbados, the Cayman Islands, and Luxembourg. This means that federal and provincial governments lose at least $7.8 billion in tax revenue every year, the association says. That's a big loss when you consider that it would cost just $4.7 billion spread over a ten-year period to provide clean drinking water and proper sanitation to First Nations communities throughout Canada.

Yet the answer is not a wealth tax. It's hard to administer and it drives the wealth creators away. As for the tax on income, wealthy people already pay more than their fair share.

Why, then, the sustained attacks on the wealthy?

It's an easy political populist win. Philip Cross, a senior fellow at the Fraser Institute, spent thirty-six years at Statistics Canada. He studied income growth slowing and, in some cases, declining between 2008 and 2016 in most countries belonging to the Organisation for Economic Co-operation and Development (OECD). Over that same time, most OECD countries saw a higher share of income accumulate to the richest 10 percent of earners. Seven of the thirty-seven member countries experienced a rare phenomenon of falling average incomes at the same time as more income went to the wealthy: Greece, Austria, the Netherlands, Belgium, Finland, Italy, and, crucially, the United States. When that rift happens, people get angry—and, as Cross puts it, that "triggers strong political pressure to increase taxes on the richest."

CANADA IS NOT LIKE THE UNITED STATES

Canada did not experience what other developed countries did: between 2007 and 2017, the share of income going to the top 10 percent *declined*. Meanwhile, their share of taxes went up! When you compare the top 10 percent's share of income taxes with their income, the income tax burden was at the highest on record since 1982. So the situation in Canada is different. Yet, Cross observes, Canadians have

> imported the overwrought rhetoric about sharply rising inequality from the United States without adjusting for the very different circumstances of high-income people in Canada. Many Canadians have been led to believe that incomes in recent years have risen only for the very rich and this hoarding explains why incomes have stalled for everyone else. Such views are entirely wrong and misleading.

The appeal of taxes on the wealthy, says Cross, is that "such policies cultivate the illusion that government services can be expanded for most people at no apparent cost to themselves. It is also dangerous politics, with its implications that upper income earners do not pay their fair share [of taxes]."

Consider how much we Canadians enjoy—and have come to expect—in terms of generous social benefits. We are the envy of much of the world. We have a high standard of living, and a highly educated and skilled workforce. We are committed to social justice and helping the needy and less fortunate. Nothing is perfect, of course. Canadians want better health care and child care, higher minimum wages, improved job guarantees, lower (or free) college and university tuition, adequate housing, jobs for the homeless, clean water and air, and we want to fight and win the battle against climate change. All good. But all that generosity costs. In fact, it costs a fortune, and someone has to pay for it. Who? To those who say the rich should pay more, may I offer a word of caution? If we impose punitive rates on millionaires and billionaires in our country, they will simply elect to leave, and we will be worse off than before. The top 10 percent of the earners in Canada pay for half of the roads, hospitals, schools, police forces, firefighters, paramedics, and so on. Without them, be prepared for half of everything we enjoy becoming unfunded.

THE RIGHT WAR, THE WRONG ENEMY

Inequality cannot be ignored, but neither should it become the false context for bad policy. Targeting the rich with punitive taxes will not benefit our society. It will, in fact, make it worse, by driving away the very people we need to pay for the services that form the bedrock of Canada's social safety system. "We all live better" today, concludes economics writer Tom Hyde, "than the once richest man in the world because the world got richer. Not because we printed more money, but because we created more wealth."

CHAPTER 5

RICH KIDS INHERITING WEALTH

When we talk about taxing the rich, it doesn't take long before the critics aim their fire at the heirs—the next generation that will inherit millions, or more. They're easy to criticize. They grow up with the connections, schools, social skills, and money that will pave their way to the top. They get the benefits of growing up in an affluent family. Sweet! So why don't we tax them out of existence?

Governments might do that for one of two reasons: to raise money or to create a more fair society. Yet as we will see, neither of those rationales makes sense.

GOVERNMENT MONEY GRAB?

Canada doesn't have an inheritance tax and hasn't had one since 1972, when it was replaced by a capital gains tax that is imposed when someone dies.

If an inheritance tax were loaded onto the current capital gains tax, that would amount to double taxation.

Even if you thought that was a good idea, what would it achieve? To what extent would it pay the government's bills?

The Canadian Centre for Policy Alternatives is calling for a tax of 45 percent on inherited wealth of CA$5 million or more, saying it would raise $2 billion a year. However, that's a trivial amount when you consider that the pandemic drove the 2020 federal deficit up to nearly $350 billion, and total debt owed by Canada to over $1.2 trillion! Even if the tax on inherited wealth were 100 percent, the revenue generated wouldn't wipe out the deficit, let alone the staggering debt. Generations of future Canadians will be paying the debt load incurred.

Different countries around the world use different kinds of taxation when someone dies, and this is not the place to review worldwide policy on this front. However, "what is surprising about these different types of wealth transfer taxes is how little revenue they raise," Toronto estate lawyer Margaret O'Sullivan wrote in an online post: "They have played an increasingly smaller role in the post-war era as governments throughout the world have turned to the broader, more immediate, and recurring bases of income, consumption, payroll and social security taxes."

DO RICH KIDS STOP OTHERS FROM RISING UP?

Even if the inheritance tax failed to raise the desired amount of money for the government, critics pull out another reason for hitting rich kids with punitive taxes: fairness. Their position is: Why should some kids have a better chance of success than others? Doesn't that inherited money effectively create a insiders' club that shuts ordinary kids out of the ladder to success?

Well, you might think that, but it's not true.

Just look at the people at the helm of Canada's biggest companies. They aren't all Old Boys from Upper Canada College. Very few of them are members of the venerable Toronto Club. As author Diane Francis has shown, the influence of great inherited wealth has declined in Canada: "Concentration of power has always been, and still remains, a characteristic of Canada because of its five powerful chartered banks who have picked winners and losers among clientele; tariff barriers that kept out competitors; and non-existent anti-trust or competition laws to keep the playing field level," Francis wrote in an e-mail to me. In her 1986 book *Controlling Interest: Who Owns Canada?*, Francis indicated that thirty-two families and five conglomerates controlled 40 percent of banking, business, and politics in Canada. The families alone owned 31 percent of the nation's 500 largest public companies. At the time, Bernie Ghert, president of Cadillac Fairview Corporation Limited, forecasted that "in a number of years, there will be six groups running the country."

It didn't happen.

One generation after her initial book, Canada was more of a meritocracy than ever, according to Francis. The reason? In her 2008 sequel *Who Owns Canada Now?*, Francis provides the stark statistics on inherited wealth.

> In 1986, only 11 of the country's 32 richest families were self-made and the rest were inheritors, but by 2007, 56 of the 75 billionaires in Canada were self-made and half were immigrants … As for public-sector economic clout, in 1987 there were $150 billion in pension funds in Canada and by 2006 there were $1.065 trillion, a sevenfold increase. In 1990, there were $137.6 billion in RRSPs, and by 2006 there were $500 billion.

She goes on to add: "A vast democratization of ownership has taken place in Canada in just two decades ... Besides having diversified ownership, the top 50 companies in 2007 were diversified geographically and sectorally, involved in energy, mining, high-tech, manufacturing, banking, insurance, telecommunications, and retail. Many were global players."

This happened because of a variety of government policies: tough, new competitions legislation; the rise of a powerful public sector through pension fund capital and Crown corporations; privatizations; and free trade with the United States.

In other words, Canada is not a country where inherited wealth acts as a barrier against newcomers. It's the reverse; newcomers are the ones who are most often making the big bucks. While newcomers are building the companies of the future, the children who inherit the wealth frequently do not rise to the top.

You might have heard the saying "shirtsleeves to shirtsleeves." Generation one makes the fortune; generation two enjoys it; and by the third generation, the money is gone. You can find the same expression around the world—rice bowl to rice bowl, clog to clog. In China, they say: "The first generation builds the wealth; the second generation lives like gentlemen; the third generation must start all over again."

It's the curse of inherited wealth, and if you look around, you'll surely find stories to illustrate it. The Vancouver millionaire's grandson who wanted to be a Hollywood movie producer and spent most of his considerable inheritance on the quest. The daughter of an investment dealer CEO who married a handsome stockbroker who made some terrible calls, leaving their grandchildren scraping for cash. The sixty-year-old son of the Toronto financier who's still living with his elderly mother. Or—even more common—the legions of pleasant young men who slip into the life of golf and fishing, and never amount to much. The curse strikes fear in the hearts of entrepreneurs who have an intense desire to keep the money in the family for future generations to benefit from.

The most frequently cited statistic comes from Roy Williams and Vic Preisser in their 2010 book, *Preparing Heirs*. Williams leads The Williams Group, which is in the business of helping wealthy families pass the money to the next generation. Its tag line is "We prepare heirs." In the book, Williams notes that by 2050, we will see "the greatest transfer of wealth the world has ever experienced."

But there's a hitch. When Williams studied 3,250 wealthy families over a twenty-year period, he found that 70 percent of wealth transitions "fail."

This statistic set off alarm bells everywhere, but what did it mean?

By "success," Williams and Preisser mean that wealth remains under the control of the beneficiaries. "Failure" means that the business is sold, the wealth is taxed away, the stocks evaporate in a crash, or the money is donated.

Williams's research suggests that most wealthy families do not maintain control of their money-spinning companies, mostly because of the psychological dynamics of the family itself. The patriarch treats the kids as not ready to manage the money and hesitates to give them control and influence in the family enterprise. Communication and trust, between siblings and between generations, starts to decline. The children are not prepared to take on the responsibility of running the family business or are not a fit for that type of role. There's no "family mission."

This problem is driving a burgeoning business called the "family office." These businesses help families with generational money or family-owned businesses prepare the heirs to take over, and not lose it all or wreck themselves in the process.

There are plenty of pitfalls in the quest to move money and responsibility on to the next generation. One big problem arises when the entrepreneur thinks his kids are simply not as smart, capable, and hard-working as he is, Dennis Jaffe writes in *Forbes* magazine. He's a clinical psychologist with a mission to "help multi-generational families to develop governance practices that build the capability of next generation leadership and ensure ongoing capability of financial organizations and family offices to serve their family clients." Jaffe goes on to write:

> Paternalism (taking care of those who are not able to take care of themselves) communicates a message to them that they can never measure up to the family legacy and are barely expected to ... Furthermore, by tapping into inheritors' uncertainty and even guilt about their good fortune—and their anxieties about finding a place where they themselves can shine—this attitude can fuel a self-fulfilling prophecy. Heirs are conditioned to be passive and not contribute, and, to nobody's surprise, that is often how they act. Given a small but significant income from a restrictive trust that asks nothing of them, they respond by acting like adult children! After all, if the trust does not view them as responsible adults, what is their motivation for acting that way?

The average life expectancy of a business being owned by the same family is fifty to sixty years, according to John L. Ward, co-founder of The Family Business Consulting Group and author or co-author of a slew of leading books on family business. "Inherited wealth can destroy entrepreneurial drive," Ward writes. "When security and affluence come too easily, the work ethic can be compromised. Success requires sacrifice—but that lesson is difficult to learn when wealth relieves the need for sacrifice. The second generation, however intelligent and educated, can fail to develop the 'fire-in-the-belly' to lead a business through the demanding challenges of change."

These consultants are writing about failure to keep the family business in the family, which is the dream of many entrepreneurs who spend a lifetime building a major business. But what about the ordinary guy who hits the jackpot?

Most lottery-ticket purchasers think that winning the big prize will be the end to work life and the beginning of a life of luxury. The opposite is true. In a 2001 study of people playing the lottery in Massachusetts in the 1980s, a trio of economists found, not surprisingly, that lottery winners worked less and spent more after the big payday. Here was the surprise, however: "After receiving about half their prize, individuals saved about 16 percent."

More statistical evidence of how hard it is to keep money comes from Jay Zagorsky, a senior lecturer at Boston University's Questrom School of Business: "In my own research, I found that the average person in their 20s, 30s and 40s who was given an inheritance or large financial gift quickly lost half the money through spending or poor investments," Zagorsky wrote in *The Conversation*. It is even possible, Zagorsky notes, to blow a billion dollars.

Take Huntington Hartford, who lived from 1911 to 2008. He "was the heir to the Great Atlantic & Pacific Tea Company fortune," Zagorsky writes in *The Conversation*.

> This company, which started just before the Civil War, is better known as the A&P supermarket chain. A&P was the first US coast-to-coast food store, and from World War I to the 1960s was what Walmart is for today's American shoppers.
>
> Hartford inherited approximately $90 million when he was 12. Adjusting for inflation means he was given more than $1.3 billion as a child, after taxes. Yet Huntington declared bankruptcy in New York in 1992, approximately 70 years after being handed one of the largest fortunes in the world.

Hartford had the reverse Midas touch. He lost millions buying real estate, creating an art museum and sponsoring theaters and shows. He combined poor business skills with an exceptionally lavish lifestyle. After declaring bankruptcy, he lived as a recluse with a daughter in the Bahamas until he died.

I share these stories to underline a key point: money is hard to keep. Clearly, it's hard to keep control over the family business, even with expert help. Most families don't. It means the grandkids may inherit some cash, but they don't have a guaranteed job as vice-president, president, or even chair of the family firm. Inherited cash or a big lottery win, as we have seen, is easy to spend. So most families that have money today, even a great deal of money, are unlikely to still have it in three generations.

Does inherited wealth matter? Surely it helps, even if you don't have a bundle of cash. You do have the family connections, the confidence, the positive outlook.

Looking back over my career, I like to think I started from scratch, but people who knew me growing up or had heard of my father or his business don't believe it. How could they? "Gimme a break! You grew up rich!" Guilty as charged, for some of the time anyway.

There is no doubt that wealth (like celebrity or fame) creates advantages and opportunities for our children that are unavailable to others, but I am convinced that those benefits are rarely decisive or permanent when it comes to creating wealth. Having a parent with a foot in the door helps, but you still have to have the talent, interest, and drive to make it work. It's why, overall, the record is not that great for the children of movie stars or great athletes. If you can't act or play the sport at a high level, it doesn't matter whose son or daughter you are. The same is true in wealth and business. You might be lucky enough to inherit the keys to the kingdom, but that won't get you very far if you can't manage it or work at the level required.

Business is a great equalizer and the best venue to eliminate prejudice and privilege. In my company, our policy on diversity, equity, and inclusion is published on our website and we live by it. We aren't interested in who a job candidate's parents are, what clubs they belong to, or which school they attended. We couldn't care less. What we want to know is: Are you potentially the best person for this job? Can you handle the effort required? Are you interested in what we do? Do you align with our company's core values of being accountable, transparent, professional, and driven?

I had a lot of advantages. My father, the second in his family to graduate from university, was a great example of just how important education is, not only for practical reasons but also for the way a university education stretches one's brain and exposes one to wider options and opportunities. Growing up, I learned that much of success is based on exposure—showing up for the unexpected left turn or whatever; the new experience that enables you to recognize the opportunity you otherwise would have missed.

It's true that as my father's son, I could see first-hand the appeal of being wealthy. I was privileged, to be sure, but the most helpful advantage I had from my dad was the living example of what it is like to take risks, make plans, and survive the ups and downs of being an entrepreneur without bailing in difficult times.

Success is hard to achieve, and to get up every day when it gets tough and to keep going, you need more than friends, family, and well-wishers. You will also need the guidance of mentors. Some people brought up with money have more connections than those who weren't; however, mentors are attracted to effort and interest. No matter how much money a person has, a mentor will not invest much if there isn't a commitment to doing the hard work to get ahead. Mentors can help you move ahead, and if you are just starting, you can hire one, like I did.

I still remember the day, on a referral from a friend, that Doug Bouey came to visit me to talk about what he did. He said he helped entrepreneurs like me grow their businesses by growing themselves. I was terrified to spend the money, and more terrified to join his group. However, in my first year, that membership paid for itself three times over with critical decisions that came from either Doug or other members of the group. I stayed with Doug for twenty-seven years, growing my business from $1 million in sales in 1994 to $518 million in sales in 2020.

The role of mentoring is invaluable during the entire career arc. You never know when you will have to hit the survival button on your business or find yourself in front of a meaningful new opportunity that is above your level of comprehension. Mentors caution us when we are betting the farm and need to pull back, and coach us when we are not stretching and taking the risks necessary to grow. Mentorship is a meaningful way that successful people help push others, through shared experiences, to reach a bit higher than they might have thought possible, to plan further ahead than they would be comfortable doing on their own.

My future business partner Larry Fichtner came into Doug's group of entrepreneurs that met monthly. Larry very successfully grew a seismic company called Veritas from a small Calgary operation to a listing on the New York Stock Exchange and one of the largest seismic companies in the world. He was fifteen years my senior, and in 2001 I asked if he would read my business plan. Two days later, Larry called with a proposal. He liked my plan and sensed that I needed help. In growing Veritas, he himself had a mentor, and he wanted to pay it forward and mentor me. He purchased 15 percent of S.i. Systems and became chair of the board. Larry changed my thinking in ways that I could have never done myself. The first order of business was to hire professionals to write a real business plan. It changed everything.

Step by step, when times were good and when they were bad, Larry and Doug were unconditional sponsors for me and my company. They added value to my thinking and success, encouraged me to take bigger steps than I would have known how to do on my own, and helped me where my experience had gaps and theirs was rich. I truly owe much of my success to these two men. And I wasn't the only one. Larry and Doug helped many aspiring entrepreneurs achieve their dreams.

Growing up in an affluent family taught me the appeal of abundance, and I knew if I wanted it in my life, I would have to work for it. It has taken me more than thirty years to get here. I know the hard work and the grit it takes to make it through bad, and good, times and the vulnerability it takes to ask for help. What I can assert unequivocally, however, is that the value of anything you inherit, be it money, land, talent, or intelligence, is worth very little if you do not put in the effort and work to steward and grow what you have been gifted by the grace of circumstance.

{ CHAPTER 6 }

SPREADING THE WEALTH

I n the middle of 2020, as the pandemic was rac-
ing around the world, black-tie fundraisers were
cancelled. But in that year, the media reported one
eye-popping donation after another. For example:

- The Rogers family announced a CA$60-million gift
  to help with the economic fallout from the health
  crisis, with the money immediately going to nine
  organizations, including food banks, shelters, and
  groups that support vulnerable children.

- Simon Fraser University alumnus Lance Uggla,
  CEO of the London-based financial data giant IHS
  Markit, announced a record CA$34-million gift
  in December to improve social mobility and access
  to higher education for students from disadvan-
  taged and minority backgrounds.

- The Garron family donated over CA$15 million
  to Toronto's Centre for Addiction and Mental Health
  (CAMH) to support research that will enhance
  understanding of the brain chemistry underlying
  mental illness.

Bill Gates, Warren Buffett, and MacKenzie Scott were
donating billions to great causes around the world.

Yet critics of the rich are not impressed. They say
most philanthropists just want to get their name on a
building or get the tax break that goes with the donation. So wealthy people are unique in at least one sense:
they are criticized for both not giving enough and giving
at all. They're selfish if they don't give. If they do give,
they're criticized for not giving more. In the early days
of the pandemic, Amazon's Jeff Bezos gave US$100 mil-
lion to American food banks and another $25 million
to a Washington State relief charity, yet he was criticized for not giving more. The *Washington Post* (which
Bezos owns) mocked his donation, noting that it was
the equivalent of a median-earning American donating
$85, even though it was the largest single gift in the
hunger relief non-profit's history. Robert Reich, former
US labor secretary and avid tax-the-rich enthusiast,
also chimed in with some incredibly incorrect math
to make a jab: "Jeff Bezos has raked in $34,600,000,000

in the last two months—346 times the $100 million donation to food banks he can't stop talking about. Billionaire philanthropy won't save us. Tax the rich."

Do the critics have a point?

In the United States, barely one-fifth of philanthropic contributions goes directly into the hands of the poor. "A lot goes to the arts, sports teams and other cultural pursuits, and half goes to education and healthcare," according Paul Vallely, an internationally acclaimed commentator on politics, religion, and society and author of *Philanthropy from Aristotle to Zuckerberg*. He is currently senior research fellow at the Global Development Institute, University of Manchester. "The biggest donations in 2019 in education went to elite universities and schools that the rich themselves attended," Vallely notes. "The common assumption that philanthropy automatically results in a redistribution of money is wrong ... A lot of elite philanthropy is about elite causes."

Some philanthropy is based on need, with exemplars of that being Jimmy Carter, Oprah Winfrey, and Bill Gates, who funds global investments in the eradication of diseases like malaria and HIV by putting together programs and initiatives that governments can't. In response, anti-wealth critics are asking: are we okay with literally a handful of super-rich men and

women making their own decisions on what causes
to support? Well, what's wrong with it? Just because
a philanthropist might have his or her own cause,
isn't every donation worth celebrating? If a Seymour
Schulich or Raymond Chang ends up with his name
across a new hospital or medical centre, aren't we all
better off? If the philanthropic donation builds a new
wing in an art museum, or supports young artists and
writers and poets, or expands much-needed mental
health services in a community, shouldn't we be happy?
Government will not—or cannot—pay for all of this.

And do you know who agrees with this view?
Critics like McQuaig might be surprised. It is former
left-of-centre NDP politicians who are now running major charities that help the poor. The story
of how they came to appreciate the massive impact
of philanthropy is told in a new book, *Lessons Learned
on Bay Street*, by one of the country's top philanthropists, Donald K. Johnson. Johnson is a major
eight-figure donor himself, and he has been fighting
for years to change Canada's tax laws to make them
more effective in stimulating charitable giving. His
advocacy campaign has already scored one major victory: Canadians can make donations of public stocks
without paying any capital gains tax. But that victory
didn't come easily.

As he lobbied the federal government, Johnson pulled in some heavy hitters like Jim Pitblado, chair of Toronto's Hospital for Sick Children; Rob Prichard, president of the University of Toronto from 1990 to 2000; Robin Cardozo, vice-president and chief executive of the United Way of Canada; and Hal Jackman, who was there as the lieutenant governor of Ontario but also chaired the Council for Business and the Arts, now known as Business/Arts.

Yet senior bureaucrats in the federal finance department created headwinds and obstacles. "They were concerned that further tax relief on charitable donations would cost the treasury hundreds of millions of dollars in lost revenues at a time when the government was facing huge deficits. They also believed that the government, not the donor, should decide which not-for-profit groups should benefit from taxpayer funding," Johnson writes.

Then Johnson got busy with a big letter-writing campaign to MPs, and it paid off. The 1997 budget cut the capital gains tax payable on a gift of securities in half. For Johnson, that was a terrific move, but he wanted to eliminate the entire capital gains tax on a gift of securities, not just cut it in half.

Not surprisingly, "the New Democratic Party was opposed because it perceived our proposal as a 'tax break for the rich,'" Johnson writes in his book. It seemed to go over their heads that the "rich" worked hard to make the money they were giving; they were not handing out anyone else's earned income, only their own.

Now Johnson, who loves to quote his motto, "The sale begins when the customer says no," made his Oscar-winning political move: he got in touch with five former NDP politicians "who came to recognize the benefits of the measure after they became involved in the not-for-profit sector."

One of those people was Frances Lankin, who had been a cabinet minister in the Bob Rae government in Ontario and was by then president of United Way Greater Toronto. Lankin agreed with Johnson that more donations of shares would be a real bonanza. As Johnson tells the story, Lankin commissioned an analysis of share donations to the United Way since its inception in 1956. It found that in the forty years from 1956 to 1996, total donations of shares amounted to only CA$44,000. But in the eight years since 1997, when the capital gains tax was halved, gifts of stock had surged to more than $24 million.

More support rolled in from Anne Swarbrick, another former minister in the Rae government who headed the Toronto Foundation. Former Toronto mayor David Miller and former Saskatchewan premier Roy Romanow signed onto Johnson's formidable lobbying campaign too.

Sure enough, the May 2006 budget included a provision removing the remaining capital gains tax on donations of publicly listed shares. Leaders in the not-for-profit sector across Canada were delighted. So was Johnson: "After a decade of hard work, our campaign had paid off."

The results have been incredible: almost every year since 2006, charities across Canada have received more than $1 billion in gifts of listed securities from individual and corporate donors.

⸻

Philanthropy is everyone's responsibility. Instead of complaining and putting the responsibility to donate on the obvious few billionaires in the news, we should be encouraging as much philanthropic generosity as possible. Everyone can donate something. Are we all in this together or not? Frankly, I commend the wealthy philanthropists for increasingly donating part of their fortune to charities; we need more of that, not less. I applaud companies that encourage employees to engage with local charities as part of their corporate commitment. We need more of that. It is better for the community and for the company and its employees. I have seen the positive effect in my own company when employees devote time to local charities. They feel invested in the communities they live in. They become responsible for outcomes. I think spending time, money, or talent like this makes us all better and more responsible citizens.

At S.i. Systems, for instance, we have a policy that, in addition to their vacation and flex days, each employee gets five volunteer days a year to donate time to any charity they choose. What has been so inspiring to me is how enthusiastic employees have been about donating their time. They like making the connections with the community and feel better for being a contributing member to their interests in the community. On a personal level, it makes me immensely proud to be associated with so many talented men and women for whom "giving back" is meaningful and not just a virtue-signalling Instagram post that took five seconds of effort.

Canadians are among the most generous citizens in the world. In my home province, for instance, Albertans donated nearly $1.6 billion in 2019, with a median donation of $500, which put the province once again at the top of all others in terms of generosity. Unfortunately the number of donors in Canada has declined over the last decade, from 5.8 million people in 2008 to 5.17 million in 2019. Despite that, total charitable giving climbed by 25 percent during that same time period, to $10.3 billion. How was that possible? Because wealthy donors have become increasingly vital to helping non-profits and charitable groups fund their operations. The wealthy are picking up the slack for the benefit of the general population.

In 2018, Canadian charities that mounted fundraising campaigns attracted 73 percent of their campaign revenue from major gifts, up from 63 percent five years earlier, according to a survey by KCI, a consultancy for the non-profit sector. More than 60 percent of those big gifts came from individuals, the rest from foundations. What's more, nearly half of fundraising revenue in 2018 was from separate donations of more than $1 million each, up from 30 percent in 2013.

Here's one other eye-popping figure that shows the growing significance of philanthropy by the wealthy to the overall charitable sector. According to figures compiled by the University of Toronto, there were only a handful of publicly announced major gifts of $5 million or more twenty years ago, and they added up to less than $25 million in total donations. By 2019, there were sixty-five of these big gifts, and they were really big: the total donation value was around $1.3 billion.

The Breadth of Giving

When we drill down to the various non-profit causes, we really begin to see how philanthropy supports the charities and non-profit organizations that enrich so many lives in this country. In the non-profit sectors highlighted here, it would be impossible to list every major donor, but a few gifts from recent years stand out for their size and importance and serve to underscore the contributions of philanthropy.

Health Care

Canada's population is rapidly aging, and that's putting increased strain on the country's health care institutions. Adjusting for inflation, health care spending in Canada has skyrocketed from CA$57 billion in 1975 to $266 billion in 2019, according to the Canadian Institute for Health Information. And that doesn't even include the shock the health care system has had to absorb from the COVID-19 pandemic. Fortunately, philanthropy has risen alongside those costs. Health care receives the second-largest share of donations from Canadians after religious organizations. According to figures from Statistics Canada, government non-profit health institutions raised just over $1.98 billion from individual donors in 2019, an increase of $356 million from 2007.

Donations are particularly important in a province like Ontario, for instance, where hospitals are responsible for covering 10 percent of the costs of big construction projects, like new wings or the installation of major diagnostics equipment, as a condition for the provincial government to provide the remaining 90 percent.

- In March 2020, Charles and Margaret Juravinski announced their latest donation to health care centres in Hamilton, a CA$100-million endowment fund for medical research at the city's three research institutions—McMaster University, Hamilton Health Sciences, and St. Joseph's Healthcare. The gift, which will be distributed by the couple's estate after they die, came on the heels of more than $50 million in other donations they'd made in the health sector. Importantly, the couple left it up to the institutions themselves to decide what research will be funded, knowing that needs will change over time. Charles, eighty-nine, who along with his eighty-eight-year-old wife developed and eventually sold the Flamboro Downs racetrack outside of Hamilton, has summed up his lifetime of philanthropy this way: "Giving is like a drug. Nothing feels better than helping others."

- Over the years, Peter Gilgan has donated more than CA$260 million to non-profits, mostly in the health care sector in and around Southwestern Ontario. The founder and CEO of residential real estate developer Mattamy Homes made his largest single donation to Toronto's Hospital for Sick Children in 2019, which was also the hospital's largest single gift ever. Unfortunately, it didn't take long for some critics to question whether the hospital should accept the money, citing the fact that Mattamy Homes was also a top donor to right-wing advocacy group Ontario Proud. Mattamy later said it regretted making the one-time donation to the group, but the episode showed that even when wealthy entrepreneurs like Gilgan step up to help vital institutions, there are those who can't get past their hostility to wealth. It's a foolish attitude given the needs of the non-profit sector.

Education

During the last decade, provincial funding for post-secondary education has stagnated, launching universities and colleges into an urgent fundraising push. Schools have long been a favourite recipient of bequests from Canada's philanthropists, many of whom seek to return the benefit they themselves received from their educations. So it's no surprise that wealthy donors have ramped up their support when universities come calling. In the ten-year period up to 2019, donations to Canadian universities and colleges from individuals jumped by almost CA$200 million to a total of $625 million. While still a small portion of schools' overall revenues, those donations have proved critical for institutions looking to expand their campuses, offer scholarships, and fund research initiatives.

- In September 2020, the University of Toronto, which has long excelled at attracting major donors, landed its largest gift ever when James and Louise Temerty donated CA$250 million to the university to fund a new centre for artificial intelligence in health care and to support under-represented students. The eighty-year-old entrepreneur and businessman who built the ComputerLand franchise into Canada's largest chain of computer stores now serves as chairman of Northland Power, a green energy company he founded in 1987. With his gift, he set a new benchmark that others are likely to follow. As David Palmer, U of T's vice-president of university advancement and head of its fundraising initiatives, told the *Globe and Mail* after the gift, "There's ample evidence that these large gifts cause others to think about what they're doing to lift their sights. I think we all feel that we have barely begun to tap the enormous financial capacity for philanthropy that exists in our society."

- The previous record for philanthropic giving in Canada had been set only a year earlier. In February 2019, John and Marcy McCall MacBain gifted CA$200 million to McGill University to fund graduate scholarship at the university from which John McCall MacBain had graduated with an economics degree in 1980. From 1987 to 2006, he was the founder and CEO of Trader Classified Media, a classified advertising company that debuted on the Nasdaq exchange in 2000 before it was sold in 2006. Today he runs Pamoja Capital, a private investment firm, from his home in Geneva. When the couple set up their family foundation in 2006, they pledged to give away 80 percent of their fortune and future income to charity. As of 2015, their net worth was estimated to be $1.4 billion so watch for more potential announcements in the years to come.

Arts and Culture

When it comes to philanthropy, there's arguably no sector more closely associated with wealthy donors than the arts. Before public funding of the sector came along, private donors were a driving force behind the creation of many of Canada's symphonies, theatres, and dance companies. US foundations like the Carnegie Foundation and the Rockefeller Foundation provided crucial early funding to the National Ballet of Canada and the Banff Centre for Arts and Creativity. In time, Canadian donors took on a larger role. In 2013, a total of CA\$160 million was raised from donors, up 52 percent from 2007, according to Statistics Canada. In the wake of the COVID-19 pandemic, which devastated the arts sectors by robbing them of crucial ticket sales, philanthropy is likely to play a significant role in helping organizations get back on their feet.

- One of the largest-ever arts donations in Canada happened in 2017, far from the nation's traditional cultural capitals. That year, Saskatoon philanthropist Ellen Remai, whose husband, Frank, along with his brothers Joe and John built one of the province's largest real estate development companies, announced the latest gift to establish the Remai Modern art gallery in the prairie city. All told, the Frank and Ellen Remai Foundation kicked in CA\$103 million since 2011 to fund the design, construction, and operation of the gallery.

- Arguably, the most significant gift seen in the arts sector continues to be the 2002 donation by billionaire Ken Thomson to the Art Gallery of Ontario before his death in 2006. The art collector gifted his CA$300-million private art collection to the AGO, along with $50 million earmarked for a renovation campaign and $20 million to the gallery's endowment fund.

Social Services

As I wrote earlier in this chapter, the pandemic motivated Canada's wealthy as well as many businesses to step up in a major way to help those impacted by the fallout from the virus and lockdown measures. Here's one way to quantify that assistance. During 2018 and 2019, roughly 14 percent of all gifts of at least CA$500,000 went to community service non-profits, but during the first six months of the pandemic, from March to August 2020, the sector saw the largest inflow of donations of any charitable sector, with 43 percent of major gifts going to community services, according to research done by KCI. Here's a sample of the types of donations that have occurred during the pandemic.

- Radio pioneer Allan Slaight has long been a major donor to various causes, including a CA$15-million gift through the Slaight Family Foundation to the United Way Greater Toronto in 2019, the charity's largest gift ever. The giving continued during COVID. In March 2020, the foundation gave $3 million to four charities focused on alleviating hunger, including Food Banks Canada and Second Harvest. A year later, the Slaight family stepped up with $30 million to support nineteen organizations in improving mental health care in Canada, including the Centre for Addiction and Mental Health.

- In April 2020, mining veteran Eric Sprott and his family's Sprott Foundation announced they were giving CA$20 million to fight hunger during the pandemic, with the money going to Community Food Centres Canada and Second Harvest. The donation called for 60 percent of the money to go to grocery gift cards, with most of the balance supporting food programs. Juliana Sprott, Eric's daughter and the foundation's chief giving officer, explained their approach to online journal *The Philanthropist*: "The original plan was to make many small [$100,000] gifts spread out over a variety of grantees, and that was very well received by our board. But then my dad approached me and said, it's going to get really, really bad. So we sat down as a family [and with our board] and said, 'to really make a dent and support our fellow citizens, it has to be a significant amount of money.'"

It's that kind of attitude—being nimble yet wildly ambitious—that makes major philanthropy such a powerful force in the non-profit sector. Like I said earlier, it's time we, as a society, stop complaining about the motives behind why the rich give away so much of their wealth and do more to encourage even more philanthropic giving in the future.

A GALLERY OF GIVING

The face of philanthropy has changed and continues to change. In this section, I present a series of profiles of some of our country's most important and innovative philanthropists, not necessarily because they are the most well-known (most are not) or the richest (ditto). Rather, because of how they are doing philanthropy. What distinguishes these individuals is, firstly, their authenticity and commitment. A few come from backgrounds and circumstances that clearly undermine the critique that wealthy people are only interested in having their egos stroked. That is certainly not true of most of them, and certainly not the ones that I am fortunate enough to know.

Secondly, they are all successful entrepreneurs, innovators, and leaders. They represent a vanguard in a new era of philanthropy, which means they are setting examples of how to share some of the resources each of us earns in our lifetime. For them, philanthropy is not merely a convenient (tax-deductible) outlet for the money they have earned. Lastly, many are forty or under in age. They represent a common thread among the wealthy, starting with Cosimo de' Medici in the Renaissance, who declared that social commitments cannot be separated out from the bottom line: what is good for business must be good for the community.

The act of giving, no matter how criticized by others who just watch, is contrary to the belief that wealth creators are selfish, out-of-touch elitists. Here are a few more examples of a new wave of philanthropy.

G. Raymond Chang

Before his death in 2014 from leukemia, Ray Chang was a well-known Toronto CEO who had donated countless millions of dollars to charity. An Order of Canada recipient, Chang was a founding partner in a small mutual fund management company that he helped build, over the years, into CI Financial, the second-largest publicly traded mutual fund company in Canada. Named the

Outstanding Philanthropist of 2010 by the Association of Fundraising Professionals–Greater Toronto Chapter, Chang was a native of the West Indies. His father was of Chinese-Jamaican heritage, while his mother was born in Guyana. The family owned and operated a successful bakery in Jamaica. Ray had an early introduction to family values. When his mother's brother died, Ray's parents adopted his five children, so Ray grew up with eleven brothers and sisters. In fact, with thirty-five cousins in total living within a few blocks of each other, the Chang family was a community of its own. Impressively, Ray's parents insisted all twelve children attend university. Ray attended university in New York and Toronto in the late 1960s and started his career in finance. But he never forgot about his roots. Among his many notable philanthropic achievements is establishing the Gladstone and Maisie Chang Chair in Teaching of Internal Medicine at the University of Toronto—named in honour of his parents. He has also contributed to the Royal Ontario Museum and the G. Raymond Chang School of Continuing Education at Ryerson University. That's not all. Chang established a fellowship for training West Indian doctors at the University Health Network in Toronto and mentored many West Indian businesses. He was also a big donor to the Centre for Addiction and Mental Health.

Jeffrey Skoll

Billionaire Jeffrey Skoll made his fortune in the dot-com sector as president of eBay Inc. In a surprise move, not long after it went public, he jumped ship. What was the point of having all this money if he couldn't do something with it? And by "do something," he meant have a positive social benefit. He calls it "impact investing." An Officer of the Order of Canada for his "commitment to social causes and innovative practice of philanthropy," Skoll put his money where his mouth was by committing to donating as much as 95 percent of his fortune to charity. His reasoning was refreshingly low key and direct: "There's really only so much that you need, or your family needs. All else is to be turned, hopefully smartly, into a benefit for the world." Several years ago, Skoll became a member of a very small elite that had donated $1 billion or more to charity. He created the Skoll Foundation in 1999, which operates in more than one hundred countries around the world and has funded investments in Canada's Indigenous communities, at-risk children in the United States, and innovative water pumps in Africa.

Aside from the obvious good Skoll is doing, it's impressive to see his insight when it came to charities. Tavia Grant interviewed Skoll for the *Globe and Mail* and captured his thinking this way:

He noticed that the best performers among those he was supporting used business skills and financial sustainability to tackle social problems in new ways. As a concept, social entrepreneurship was still evolving, but he embraced it—and took a novel approach to fostering its growth by providing long-term funding and freedom to innovate rather than annual grants tied to specific conditions.

Grant quotes Skoll:

"Me being an entrepreneur, I realized—that's the surest way to stifle innovation. So we decided to focus on social entrepreneurs in the field, make long-term unconditional grants to them and their organizations, connect them together so they could have opportunities to meet and share and collaborate (in his annual Skoll World Forum) and to tell their stories … to inspire others."

THE VANGUARD OF THE NEW PHILANTHROPY

When Nav Bhatia arrived in Canada in 1984, it was tough: "I faced a lot of discrimination because of the way I looked," Bhatia told canadianimmigrant.ca. "It was very difficult landing a job, but I never got angry. Whatever work I did, I made sure I was the best at it.

My first job was as a landscaper and I was the proudest Canadian landscaper, I can guarantee you that." Nav Bhatia, a proud Sikh, owns two Toronto-area car dealerships and has become beloved in the city as an ambassador of positive change for the community— especially when it comes to racial discrimination. One of his early jobs was as a car salesman. A Caucasian customer refused to deal with him. "I could have been upset, but instead I stayed calm and made a deal with the next salesperson—he could do the deal, but I would get to deliver the car." The customer came back to pick up his new car, and Bhatia turned on the charm. It worked. That customer became a fan for life. "There are lots of speed bumps along the way, but you have to stay positive," he says. "That moment reinforced the personal philosophy I've followed ever since: treat people how you want to be treated yourself." A huge basketball fan, he launched the Nav Bhatia Superfan Foundation and is building basketball courts and hosting camps for kids "from all backgrounds to come together through the game of basketball."

Nav Bhatia has done very well for himself, but he wants to do well by his community, too, and while he and Jeffrey Skoll don't occupy the same rung on the financial ladder, both share a very similar commitment to what it will take to make a better world.

———◦◦◦◦———

Kyle Braatz is chief executive office and co-founder of the interactive health company Fullscript, based in Ottawa, which describes its mission as "pushing [for] wellness that is affordable and achievable and available to all ... It drives everything we do. We've got a long way to go, but every little push takes us closer to our vision of wellness fulfilled." A recipient of the Telfer School of Management (University of Ottawa) Young Achiever's Award and a two-time BNN Bloomberg Canada's Top 40 Leaders Under 40 honouree, Braatz is a great example of a young leader for whom business goals and social concerns are aligned. In support of a non-profit he founded in 2009, he raised more than CA$150,000 for cancer research by cycling more than 8,000 kilometres across Canada. A second charity founded in honour of a friend has raised more than $1.2 million.

———◦◦◦◦———

A well-known star in the Calgary business world as the founder and CEO of Minhas Micro Brewery, the tenth-largest brewery in the world, and as a Dragon in the popular TV show, Manjit Minhas was born and raised in Calgary and admits her "taste" for the brewery business began early, as her parents owned the largest liquor retailer in Calgary at the time. When she was nineteen, she and her brother launched their first beer. They had $10,000 and no business experience, so even with powerful parents in the liquor retailing business, you have to give them credit. Said Minhas: "The reason why entrepreneurs make up 1 per cent of the population is because we are willing to do what 99 per cent of the other people are not willing to do."

Besides being the best and most successful business leader she can be, Minhas is passionate about mentoring other women to do the same. "We can support women entrepreneurs by investing in them and treating them with honesty." One of her fundamentals is the idea of "sustainable change," which she tells her mentees is accomplished through "education of women entrepreneurs" and skills development, like "how to build a network, how to market your business, how to grow your business and more." Train women as entrepreneurs the same way as men. They have everything they need, in other words. All they need are the tools. Manjit's philanthropic endeavours include donating millions of dollars and volunteering to support many charities in her hometown Calgary and her parents' hometown in India.

Giving Back

When our kids were growing up, my wife and I made it a priority that we would spend our money on meaningful experiences, not possessions. Did we ever get push-back? Yes, we did. Our kids learned to make what they had last and to get the best use out of what they owned. We also supported hard work. This was our meaningful exchange of energy. If you had a passion and wanted to put in the work to explore and excel in it, we would support it. Most parents can and will support their children who want to excel in hockey, dance, music, or any other pursuit. We are very happy that we had the financial ability to support their passions, and we did so as long as the effort was there. We support causes both as individuals and as family. When it is a cause undertaken by the family, we all have to agree. When it is personal, we can each do what we want. What we especially like about the family approach is that our kids realized early that it isn't just about money; you can donate your time and talents just as easily. They found the causes, did research, figured out who or what needed help and what kind of help. It might be money; it could be time. They became more involved and invested in the outcome. It wasn't about writing a cheque and walking away. When we do contribute, it must be more than just money. To be honest, the issue of a contribution being tax deductible has never been a consideration. If it qualifies, fine, but that isn't what counts. Many of our contributions are private or outside of Canada and are not eligible for tax receipts anyway. Not that we don't like tax deductions—we do, but that doesn't influence our decisions. Last year we contributed to Toronto Hospital for Sick Children (my company matched the donation), and a few years ago my wife raised $384,000 to do fifty pediatric heart surgeries in India with the Sri Narayani Hospital & Research Centre in Tamil Nadu (we funded several hundred cataract surgeries as well). We donate annually in our local communities in Calgary, Toronto, and Halfmoon Bay.

I admit that we are very proud that our children continue to think hard about how to give back, and not in the flashy "look at me" way. Our son was part of Dancers for Cancer, a group of twelve young people who raised $1 million for Toronto's SickKids hospital. During the COVID-19 pandemic, he made a hundred bag lunches—sandwich, fruit, juice—on Tuesdays and handed them out to the homeless people on the streets in his Leslieville neighbourhood. One of our daughters is a two-time Juno nominee with six albums to date, and she volunteers her time with schools to discuss mental

health and bullying. She focuses on encouraging the
kids to keep their aspirational dreams alive.

CONCLUSION

At the end of 2019, capitalism itself was on trial in the Munk Debates in Toronto. The motion was "The capitalist system is broken. It's time to try something different." On the Yes side, Yanis Varoufakis, former Greek finance minister and star of Europe's socialist movement, argued that capitalism is immoral and corrupt. The defence starred the former head of the American Enterprise Institute, Arthur C. Brooks. He and his partner, columnist David Brooks, won by a margin of two points, and his argument, which he summarized in an interview in the *National Post*, is worth reading.

Free enterprise, a system that allows markets to allocate resources, has given the world more opportunity and less poverty, Brooks said. The five forces of prosperity—globalization, free trade, property rights, the rule of law, and the culture of entrepreneurship—have created jobs and lifted millions of people worldwide out of poverty. It requires competition to work and good public policy to allow competition.

Brooks goes on to say: "The greatest achievement of capitalism … is creating a largesse where we can have a social welfare state that provides for people and their needs."

I agree: how much wealth a successful entrepreneur can make in a lifetime of work has a direct and beneficial effect on lifting the wealth of others in our communities and nations. Removing the rich from a community or country increases poverty, decreases services, and increases costs for everyone. Wealth creators—entrepreneurs—have given their societies a host of benefits that have increased our standard of living.

I've argued that the most effective way to create jobs, reduce poverty, shrink income disparities, and raise living standards is by growing the economy. Making the pie bigger instead of fighting over who gets the biggest slice of a smaller pie. To do this, societies need to understand that entrepreneurs and companies are the wealth creators; governments only redistribute wealth. If you want a higher standard of living for everyone, if you want to raise the poorest among us out of poverty, you need more rich people in your nation, not fewer.

We need to accept that there are rewards for everyone in the hard work and significant risk entrepreneurs take. Competition is a good thing—in school, in sports, and in business. It brings out the best in us.

What can government do to increase the wealth of the general population?

We are embarking on the fourth industrial revolution, driven by science and technology. Each preceding industrial revolution required a better-educated workforce. Each brought greater market competition and new opportunity for wealth creators to lift their communities and their country as a whole. The wealth creators reduced poverty, raised living standards, and created more meaningful jobs for the general population.

Successful governments in each evolution had a critical duty to help individuals gain access to the benefits of the new industrial revolution. They did it through education, a fair judicial system that recognized corporate and individual rights, open trade policies, and competitive taxation. It is an ongoing process, throughout life, as careers and jobs change and adapt to dramatically new landscapes. Today, countries must compete for the ability to nurture and retain wealth creators.

It is essential in any nation to give all people equal opportunity to succeed. Without a fair playing field, you won't have an abundance of wealth creators or the benefits they bring.

Build Infrastructure

Governments can create more opportunities for everyone by building a reliable infrastructure—from rail and roads to telecommunications, education, and health care.

I wouldn't have been able to build a company like mine—supplying IT professionals—in a country with no roads or schools or hospitals. A billionaire like Mark Zuckerberg relied on the invention of the Internet, which required the invention of the computer, which relied on brilliant innovators like Alan Turing, who themselves attended universities, which were built by countless masons and electricians and staffed by … well, you get the idea.

Critics will tell you that taxpayers paid for that infrastructure, so successful entrepreneurs owe them a sizable percentage of their winnings. "The accumulation of wealth is always the fruit of a social process," Piketty writes in his book. It depends, among other things, on public infrastructure (such as legal, fiscal, and education systems), the social division of labour, and the knowledge accumulated by humanity over centuries. "Under such circumstances, it is perfectly logical that people who have accumulated large amounts of wealth should return a fraction of it to the community each year."

Yet governments did not create infrastructure without wealth creators. In fact, governments have had a long and successful partnership with them to establish infrastructure. In Canada, for instance, look at the wealth creators who built the nation—such as Canadian Pacific Railway, Hudson's Bay Company, TransCanada PipeLines, CTV, Toronto Dominion Bank, Eaton's, and Rogers. Much of our infrastructure was created by wealth creators when government wouldn't or couldn't imagine the next step. Wealth creators fill the gap when governments can't or won't.

Infrastructure—health care systems, education, roads, rail lines—are necessary for companies like mine to build and create jobs. Governments want to attract wealth creators and their businesses. They want people like me to take risks with my own time and money and hopefully spread the benefits to thousands of people each year. The payoff, for government, is vibrant communities, citizens doing meaningful work, and broader tax revenues not only from the businesses but also from the people working in them.

KEEP TAXES GLOBALLY COMPETITIVE

Today, if the Canadian government approved the NDP's hit-the-rich tax, it would pay for the government budget for—wait for it—one and a half weeks. That's right. According to the Parliamentary Budget Officer, the NDP's "super-wealth tax" could fetch the government CA$5.6 billion in its first year (rising to $9.5 billion after ten years), while the 2021 federal budget clocked in at nearly $500 billion. But what would be the full price? As we've seen in this book, wealth creators are mobile. Thousands of them left France and the United Kingdom when those nations hiked their taxes on the rich. France made US$26 billion on the wealth tax but lost over 1 trillion in the process as the rich made their exit. When George H.W. Bush implemented a luxury tax, people bought fewer high-end items, like cars, planes, and boats, and national manufacturing businesses and their employees suffered, until President Clinton repealed the tax. Nations must encourage companies and entrepreneurs to stay and grow within their borders. To do this, it's crucial to ensure that high tax rates do not push wealth creators toward putting their time and money to work in other national jurisdictions.

ENCOURAGE OPEN TRADE

Finally, to really provide open opportunity, get rid of internal and international trade barriers that stop people from crossing borders to work. International free trade agreements have contributed to considerable economic growth in Canada. One of the national ironies is that the federal and provincial governments have failed to substantially phase out internal trade barriers. "Mind-boggling rules, dueling bureaucracies and maddening regulations are estimated currently to sap billions of dollars from the Canadian economy each year," according to the Standing Senate Committee on Banking, Trade and Commerce. The gains from removing these barriers would be immense. A 2019 paper by the International Monetary Fund estimated that getting rid of internal trade restrictions would boost real GDP per capita in Canada by 3.8 percent. Fewer trade barriers means more competition, more opportunity, better efficiencies, and more wealth created.

REDUCE GOVERNMENT SPENDING
TO A REASONABLE LEVEL

Just as no amount of exercise can compensate for overeating, no amount of wealth creation can overtake unlimited government spending. History is filled with examples of countries that overspent without any regard for fiscal responsibility. Throughout the 1990s, the Argentine government chronically overspent to buy political support and prop up unproductive industries, until 2001, when it defaulted on US$90 billion of debt and plunged the country into a decade-long depression. In Greece, the 2008 recession brought an abrupt end to the country's reliance on cheap and easy credit, which had enabled it to lavishly overspend on government programs and public-sector salaries. The resulting financial crisis triggered a painful era of austerity. The debt crisis had a lasting effect, with many young people fleeing the country for work, leading to population declines every year since, while the country's unemployment rate in 2019 is still more than double what it was in 2008. Canadians don't have to look far to see the consequences of reckless, unrestrained spending—years of deficits through the 1970s, '80s, and early '90s brought Canada to the fiscal brink. After Canada experienced its first credit rating downgrade, the government was forced to reverse course and impose tough austerity measures that saw spending slashed, hospitals and schools closed, and tens of thousands of public-sector workers laid off. It's worth noting that Canada's deficit-to-GDP after the COVID pandemic is nearly three times larger than it was leading up to the 1990s fiscal crisis.

Government spending into debt is like a person overusing a credit card. At some point, lenders will stop loaning the nation money, and when that happens, watch out. Governments will need to raise money to pay the bills through higher taxes, but if they target the rich, a lot of wealth creators will move their money out the country. Then it will be up to the average person to bear the staggering load of earning a living in a bankrupt nation.

CANADA NEEDS MORE ONE-PERCENTERS

In a politically charged climate where a great many politicians and media are painting one-percenters like me as selfish people who are bad for society, I hold that the reverse is true. We need and want more one-percenters to keep our standard of living high for us, for our children, and for their children. We should celebrate organizations that employ hundreds, thousands, or even hundreds of thousands of people. As we've seen, entrepreneurs pay more than their share of taxes, and their employees pay taxes too. Wealth creators give back—big time. To hunt them until they leave the country is counterproductive: wealth creators of the future will go somewhere else to establish their companies, where those friendlier nations will redistribute the wealth they create. Those who can create wealth for themselves and the communities in which they live can easily take it to jurisdictions that want them.

So how do we continue to raise people up and create meaningful work for those who wish to work? By creating more wealth creators. The fact is, we can't live the way we live without rich people in our society. We can argue the fine print until the proverbial cows come home, but we cannot pretend for a second that capitalism hasn't been the single most important, transformational, and reliable engine for the greatest and most universally beneficial advances in human history.

Remember the calculator? A basic Hewlett-Packard calculator back in the 1970s was a cumbersome desk-top model that would have set you back a couple hundred bucks or so. It wasn't long before compact calculators as small as credit cards but with triple the computing power were being given away. Today, calculators exist primarily as free apps on a smartphone. What we need to remember is that wealth creation isn't only about increasing the money we have; it's about being able to buy (or consume) a great deal more with the money we already have.

The average Canadian has at his or her fingertip marvels of innovation and luxuries that a billionaire like Rockefeller or Carnegie could never buy a hundred years ago. Smartphones, smart cars, home entertainment on demand, exotic foods, fruit in winter—unimaginable fifty years ago. Most of us are healthier, safer, and better educated and live longer and more productive lives because of wealth creator innovations that essentially cost us nothing. We enjoy gardens, art galleries, museums, and other cultural attractions, with most of the bills paid by the state or by our wealthy citizens.

Whether or not we want to admit it, we all enjoy wealth "benefits"—passively or directly—whatever our income. A constantly improving standard of living for all is what wealth creation "gives back" every day.

We should stop thinking of the differences in wealth as an obstacle that separates us. What's wrong with a billion-dollar idea? We all benefit if and when it becomes reality. The triumph of our capitalist system is that it doesn't limit how high we want to climb. While that may mean a few at the very top are doing better than others, it doesn't mean the others are worse off. The opposite, in fact, is true.

REFERENCES

Adams, James. 2002. "Thomson Hands AGO $370-Million Donation." *Globe and Mail*, November 20, 2002. www.theglobeandmail.com/news/national/ thomson-hands-ago-370-milliondonation/ article25426249/.

Alvarez, Jorge, Ivo Krznar, and Trevor Tombe. 2019. "International Trade in China: Case for Liberalization." IMF Working Paper No. 19/158, July 22, 2019. www.imf.org/en/Publications/WP/Issues/2019/07/22/ Internal-Trade-in-Canada-Case-for-Liberalization-47100.

Anderson, Sarah. 2016. "The Failure of Bill Clinton's CEO Pay Reform." The Agenda, August 31, 2016. www.politico.com/agenda/ story/2016/08/bill-clinton-ceo-pay-reform-000195/.

Aronoff, Craig E., and John L. Ward. n.d. "Shirtsleeves to Shirtsleeves." The Family Business Consulting Group. Accessed September 6, 2021. www.thefbcg.com/ resource/shirtsleeves-to-shirtsleeves/.

Asen, Elke. 2020. "Wealth Taxes in Europe." Tax Foundation, December 17, 2020. https://taxfoundation. org/wealth-taxes-in-europe-2020/.

ATB Financial. 2019. "What Manjit Minhas Wants Entrepreneurs to Know." ATB Financial, March 12, 2019. www.atb.com/business/good-advice/start-up-business/ what-manjit-minhas-wants-entrepreneursto-know.

Benay, Alex. 2017. *Canadian Failures: Stories of Building toward Success.* Toronto: Dundurn Toronto. https://construccion.uv.cl/docs/textos/coleccion02/Texto.05.FallasCanadienses.pdf.

Boadway, Robin, and Peter Pestieau. 2019. "Over the Top: Why an Annual Wealth Tax for Canada Is Unnecessary." C.D. Howe Institute, June 2019. www.cdhowe.org/sites/default/files/attachments/research_papers/mixed/Commentary%20546.pdf.

BrainBuzz. 2020. CAMH Newsletter, November 2020. www.camh.ca/-/media/files/brainbuzz-newsletter/brain-buzz-nov2020-pdf.pdf.

Burkhauser, Richard V., Kevin Corinth, James Elwell, and Jeff Larrimore. 2020. "Evaluating the Success of President Johnson's War on Poverty: Revisiting the Historical Record Using a Full-Income Poverty Measure." Finance and Economics Discussion Series (FEDS), January 2020.

Canadian Immigrant. n.d. "Nav Bhatia." Canadian Immigrant. Accessed September 6, 2021. https://canadianimmigrant.ca/canadas-top-25-immigrants/canadas-top-25-immigrants-2018/nav-bhatia.

Canadians for Tax Fairness. n.d. "Canadian $$ in Tax Havens Reach $199 Billion." Accessed September 6, 2021. www.taxfairness.ca/en/news/canadian-tax-havens-reach-199-billion.

CBC News. 2009. "Charitable Donations Down 5.3% in 2008." CBC, November 16, 2009. www.cbc.ca/news/canada/charitable-donations-down-5-3-in-2008-1.823951.

CBC News. 2017. "Remai Family Sets Aside Another $50M for Saskatoon Art Gallery." CBC, October 20, 2017. www.cbc.ca/news/canada/saskatoon/remai-family-another-50-million-modern-gallery-1.4365278.

CBS This Morning. 2015. "Lululemon Founder on Past Controversy, New Family Business." CBS News, December 8, 2015. www.cbsnews.com/news/kit-and-ace-lululemon-founder-chip-wilson-apology-shannon-jj-retail-revolution-technical-cashmere/.

Chin, Jessica. 2018. "Canada's Richest Families Have as Much Wealth as 12 Million People." *Huffington Post*, July 31, 2018. www.huffingtonpost.ca/2018/07/31/canada-income-inequality-ccpa_a_23493121/.

Clark, James C. 2013. "The Day JFK Died, Walt Disney Discovered Orlando." *Orlando Sentinel*, November 21, 2013. www.orlandosentinel.com/opinion/os-xpm-2013-11-21-os-ed-disney-propertyanniversary-112113-20131120-story.html.

Corcoran, Terence. 2019. "Is Capitalism Broken? Terence Corcoran Interviews Arthur C. Brooks ahead of Munk Debate Appearance." *National Post*, December 3, 2019. https://nationalpost.com/opinion/is-capitalism-broken-terence-corcoran-interviews-arthur-c-brooks.

Cross, Philip. 2020. *Should Upper-Income Canadians Pay More Income Tax?* Vancouver: Fraser Institute.

Edwards, Chris, and Ryan Bourne. 2019. "Exploring Wealth Inequality." Cato Institute, November 5, 2019. www.cato.org/policy-analysis/exploring-wealth-inequality.

Fontevecchia, Agustino. 2014. "There Are More
Self-Made Billionaires in the Forbes 400 than
Ever Before." *Forbes*, October 3, 2014. www.
forbes.com/sites/afontevecchia/2014/10/03/
there-are-more-selfmade-billionaires-in-the-forbes-400-
than-ever-before/?sh=149399453369.

Food Banks Canada. 2020. "The Slaight Family
Foundation Donates over $3,000,000 to Support Food
Insecure Canadians during COVID-19 Crisis." Food
Banks Canada, March 31, 2020. www.newswire.ca/
news-releases/the-slaight-family-foundation-donates-
over-3-000-000-tosupport-food-insecure-canadians-
during-covid-19-crisis-898448060.html.

Forbes. n.d. "#574 Chip Wilson." Accessed
September 3, 2021. www.forbes.com/profile/
chip-wilson/?sh=5ab405137068.

Fox, Justin. 2014. "Piketty's 'Capital' in a Lot Less
than 696 Pages." *Harvard Business Review*,
April 24, 2014. https://hbr.org/2014/04/
pikettys-capital-in-a-lot-less-than-696-pages.

Francis, Diane. 1986. *Controlling Interest: Who Owns
Canada*. Toronto: Macmillan of Canada.

Francis, Diane. 2008. *Who Owns Canada Now? Old Money,
New Money and the Future of Canadian Business*.
Toronto: HarperCollins.

Friesen, Joe. 2020. "University of Toronto Medical School
    to Get Record $250-Million Donation." *Globe and Mail*,
    September 24, 2020. www.theglobeandmail.com/
    canada/article-university-of-torontomedical-school-
    to-get-record-250-million/.

Friesen, Joe. 2021. "University 'Mega' Donations of More
    than $10-Million Are on the Rise." *Globe and Mail*,
    January 24, 2021. www.theglobeandmail.com/canada/
    article-university-mega-donations-ofmore-than-
    10-million-are-on-the-rise/.

Gatehouse, Jonathon. 2019. "Middle-Class Mystery:
    Did Their Taxes Go Up or Down?" CBC,
    September 14, 2019. www.cbc.ca/news/politics/
    middle-class-tax-cut-fact-check-1.5283092.

Grant, Tavia. 2012. "Meet the Billionaire
    Who's Giving It All Away." *Globe and Mail*, May 26,
    2012. www.theglobeandmail.com/news/nataional/
    meet-the-billionaire-whos-giving-it-allaway/
    article4209888.

Henderson, David R. 2018. "Income Inequality Isn't The
    Problem." Hoover Institution. www.hoover.org/research/
    income-inequality-isnt-problem.

Hobson, Will, and Roxanne Roberts. 2020. "What
    the 50 Richest Americans Have Given for
    COVID-19 Relief." *The Washington Post*, June 4, 2020.
    www.washingtonpost.com/lifestyle/style/what-the-50-
    richest-americans-have-given-for-covid-19-relief/
    2020/06/02/bb70b94c-9a10-11ea-ac72-3841fcc9b35f_
    story.html.

Howe, Travis, Sameeksha Desai, and Hayden Murray. 2021. "2020 New Employer Business Indicators in the United States: National and State Trends." Kauffman Indicators of Entrepreneurship, April 2021, https://indicators.kauffman.org/wp-content/uploads/sites/2/2021/05/2020-New-Employer-Business-Indicators-in-the-United-States_April2021.pdf.

Imbens, Guido W., Donald B. Rubin, and Bruce I. Sacerdote. 2001. "Estimating the Effect of Unearned Income on Labor Earnings, Savings, and Consumption: Evidence from a Survey of Lottery Players." *American Economic Review*, 91 (4) (2001): 778–794. www.aeaweb.org/articles?id=10.1257/aer.91.4.778.

Jaffe, Dennis. 2019. "The 'Shirtsleeves-To-Shirtsleeves' Curse: How Family Wealth Can Survive It." *Forbes*, January 28, 2019. www.forbes.com/sites/dennisjaffe/2019/01/28/the-shirtsleeves-to-shirtsleeves-curse-how-family-wealth-can-survive-it/?sh=3d714bd-96c8d.

Johnson, Donald K. 2021. *Lessons Learned on Bay Street.* Toronto: Barlow Books.

Johnson, Lyndon Baines. 1964. "First State of the Union Address." January 8, 1964. www.americanrhetoric.com/speeches/lbj1964stateoftheunion.htm.

Kahloon, Idrees. 2020. "Thomas Piketty Goes Global." *New Yorker*, March 2, 2020. www.newyorker.com/magazine/2020/03/09/thomas-piketty-goes-global.

Khan, Ibrahim. 2020. "Don't Believe the Hype.
Wealth Taxes Are Nothing New." *Foreign Policy*,
August 14, 2020. https://foreignpolicy.com/2020/08/14/
wealth-tax-zakat-islamic-ancient-greece-inequality/.

Kiel, Paul, and Dan Nguyen. 2009. "Bailout Tracker."
ProPublica, April 15, 2009. https://projects.propublica.
org/bailout/.

Kirby, Jason. 2020. "What's Next for Peter Gilgan?"
Chartered Professional Accountants Canada,
May 6, 2020. www.cpacanada.ca/en/news/
pivot-magazine/2020-05-06-peter-gilgan-interview.

Kish, Matthew. 2016. "The Knight Files: 10 Business
Lessons from the Lawsuit That Gave Birth to Nike."
Portland Business Journal, April 18, 2016. www.biz-
journals.com/portland/blog/threads_and_laces/2016/04/
the-knight-files10-businesslessons-from-the.html.

Love Money. n.d. "Entire Towns and Cities Dominated
by One Company." Love Money. Accessed September 5,
2021. www.lovemoney.com/gallerylist/88848/entire-
towns-and-cities-dominated-by-one-company.

Luna, Jenny. 2019. "Phil Knight, MBA '62: Never Give Up."
Insights by Stanford Business, August 28, 2019. www.
gsb.stanford.edu/insights/phil-knight-mba-62-never-give.

Maclean's. 2019. "Jagmeet Singh's Post-Election Speech:
Full Transcript." *Maclean's*, October 22, 2019.
www.macleans.ca/politics/transcript-jagmeet-
singhs-post-election-speech/.

McArthur, Keith. 2006. "Classifieds King Finds
Riches in Charity." *Globe and Mail*, May 11, 2006.
www.theglobeandmail.com/report-on-business/
classifieds-king-finds-riches-incharity/article25677359/.

McNish, Jacquie, and Sean Silcoff. 2016. *Losing the Signal:
The Spectacular Rise and Fall of BlackBerry*. Toronto:
HarperCollins.

Mercer, Caroline. 2019. "Do the Politics or Business
Background of Health Care Philanthropists Matter?"
CMAJ News, July 31, 2019. https://cmajnews.
com/2019/07/31/do-the-politics-or-business-background-
of-health-care-philanthrophists-matter/.

Miller, Terry, Anthony B. Kim, and James M. Roberts.
2021. *2021 Index of Economic Freedom*. Washington:
The Heritage Foundation. www.heritage.org/index/
pdf/2021/book/index_2021.pdf.

Mishel, Lawrence, and Jessica Schieder. 2018. "CEO
Compensation Surged in 2017." Economic Policy
Institute, August 16, 2018. www.epi.org/publication/
ceo-compensation-surged-in-2017/.

Mishel, Lawrence, and Julia Wolfe. 2019. "CEO
Compensation Has Grown 940% since 1978." Economic
Policy Institute, August 14, 2019. www.epi.org/
publication/ceo-compensation-2018/.

MoMA. n.d. "Art and Artists: James Dyson—Dual Cycle
Vacuum Cleaner (model DCO2)." Accessed September 3,
2021. www.moma.org/collection/works/88172.

Moore, Molly. 2006. "Old Money, New Money Flee France and Its Wealth Tax." *Washington Post*, July 16, 2006. www.washingtonpost.com/archive/politics/2006/07/16/ old-money-new-money-flee-franceand-its-wealth-tax /49ac2ec7-c1b2-423e-a89b-699750275cd4/.

Murphy, Hannah, and Mark John. 2014. "France Waves Discreet Goodbye to 75 Percent Super-Tax." Reuters, December 23, 2014. www.reuters.com/article/ us-france-supertax-idUSKBN0K11CC20141223.

NDP. 2020. "We Need a Wealth Tax Now: New Democrats." NDP Newsroom, June 19, 2020. www.ndp.ca/news/ we-need-wealth-tax-now-new-democrats.

Nelson, Jacqueline, and Anna Nicolaou. 2014. "CI Financial Co-Founder G. Raymond Chang Was a Legend." *Globe and Mail*, July 28, 2014. www.the-globeandmail.com/report-on-business/streetwise/ cifinancial-co-founder-g-raymond-chang-dies-at-65/ article19814084/.

OECD. n.d. "The OECD Risks That Matter Survey." Accessed September 6, 2021. www.oecd.org/social/ risks-that-matter.htm.

Office of the Parliamentary Budget Officer. 2019. "Cost Estimate of Election Campaign Proposal." Office of the Parliamentary Budget Officer, September 10, 2019. www.pbo-dpb.gc.ca/web/default/files/Documents/ ElectionProposalCosting/Results/32630202_EN.pdf.

Picchi, Aimee. 2020. "Amazon Says It Now Has Over
    1 Million Employees." CBS News, October 30, 2020.
    www.cbsnews.com/news/amazon-1-million-employees/.

Picot, Garnett, and Anne-Marie Rollin. 2019. "Immigrant
    Entrepreneurs as Job Creators: The Case of Canadian
    Private Incorporated Companies." Statistics
    Canada, April 24, 2019. www150.statcan.gc.ca/n1/
    pub/11f0019m/11f0019m2019011-eng.htm.

Piketty, Thomas. 2014. *Capital in the Twenty-First Century*.
    Cambridge: Belknap Press.

Postmedia News. 2013. "Majority of Canada's Millionaires
    Are Self-Made and Almost Half of Them Are
    Immigrants, Poll Shows." *National Post*, June 13, 2013.
    https://nationalpost.com/news/canada/most-ofcanadas-
    millionaires-are-self-made-and-almost-half-of-them-are-
    newcomers-poll-shows.

Reich, Robert (@RBReich). 2021. "Jeff Bezos Has Raked in
    $34,600,000,000 in the Last Two Months—346 Times
    the $100 Million Donation to Food Banks He Can't Stop
    Talking about. Billionaire Philanthropy Won't Save Us.
    Tax the Rich." Twitter, May 21, 2021, 6:53 PM. https://
    twitter.com/rbreich/status/1263603786771099648?lang
    =en.

Reuters Staff. 2012. "Factbox: Venezuela's Nationalizations
    under Chavez." Reuters, October 7, 2012. www.reuters.
    com/article/us-venezuela-election-nationalizations-idUS-
    BRE89701X20121008.

Rogers. 2020. "Rogers Family Donates $60 Million to Help
Most Vulnerable Canadians Dealing with the Economic
Fallout from the COVID-19 Pandemic." Rogers,
June 15, 2020. https://about.rogers.com/newsideas/
rogers-family-donates-60-million-to-help-most-
vulnerable-canadians-dealing-with-the-economicfall-
out-from-the-covid-19-pandemic/.

Rose, Michel. 2017. "Macron Fights 'President
of the Rich' Tag after Ending Wealth Tax." Reuters,
October 3, 2017. www.reuters.com/article/
uk-france-tax-idUKKCN1C82DG.

Second Harvest. 2020. "The Sprott Foundation Makes
Transformational $20 Million Donation to Fight Hunger
during COVID-19 Pandemic." Second Harvest, April 28,
2020. www.newswire.ca/newsreleases/the-sprott-
foundation-makes-transformational-20-million-
donation-to-fight-hunger-duringcovid-19-pandemic-
822933929.html.

Senate of Canada. 2016. *Tear Down These Walls:
Dismantling Canada's Internal Trade Barriers.* Report
of the Standing Senate Committee on Banking, Trade
and Commerce, June 2, 2016. https://sencanada.
ca/content/sen/committee/421/banc/rms/2jun16/
NewsRelease-e.htm.

Silcoff, Sean. 2021. "Shopify Joins Ranks of Canada's Most
Profitable Companies with Second Windfall Quarter
as Revenues Top US$1-Billion." *Globe and Mail,*
July 28, 2021. www.theglobeandmail.com/business/
article-shopifys-side-hustle-of-backing-partner-
companiespays-off-with-fifth/.

Small Business & Entrepreneurship Council. n.d. "Facts and Data on Small Business Entrepreneurship." Small Business & Entrepreneurship Council. Accessed September 5, 2021. https://sbecouncil.org/about-us/facts-and-data/.

Sodha, Sonia. 2020. "Politicians Should Stop Bashing the Rich ... Most of Us Just Don't Agree." *Guardian*, February 16, 2020. www.theguardian.com/commentisfree/2020/feb/16/labour-should-stopdemonising-the-rich-most-britons-like-them.

Stastna, Kazi. 2011. "Clean Running Water Still a Luxury on Many Canadian Reserves." CBC, November 30, 2011. www.cbc.ca/news/canada/clean-running-water-still-a-luxury-on-many-native-reserves-1.1081705.

Tanzi, Alexandre, and Ben Steverman. 2020. "Richest New Yorkers Will Devastate City if They Leave with $133 Billion." Bloomberg, November 11, 2020. www.bloomberg.com/news/articles/2020-11-11/richest-1-in-new-york-earning-133-billion-will-devastate-city-if-they-leave.

Turley, Jonathan. 2019. "Democrats Demonize Wealthy to Deflect from Disastrous Agendas." The Hill, August 3, 2019. https://thehill.com/opinion/finance/456037-democrats-demonize-wealthy-to-deflect-from-disastrous-agendas.

TVO. 2020. "Transcript: Should Billionaires Be Taxed Out of Existence?" TVO, January 20, 2020. www.tvo.org/transcript/2594191/should-billionaires-be-taxed-out-of-existence.

Vallely, Paul. 2020. "How Philanthropy Benefits
the Super-Rich." *Guardian*, September 8, 2020.
www.theguardian.com/society/2020/sep/08/
how-philanthropy-benefits-the-super-rich.

Watt, Jaime. 2021. "Trudeau's Luxury Tax May Not
Be a Bad Idea, But Let's Not Pretend It Is Anything
More Than Showbiz." *Toronto Star*, April 25, 2021.
www.thestar.com/opinion/contributors/2021/04/25/
trudeaus-luxury-tax-may-not-be-a-bad-ideabut-lets-not-
pretend-it-is-anything-more-than-showbiz.html.

Wells, Victoria. 2021. "Posthaste: Shopify's Tobi Lutke
Is Canada's Second Richest Person—But Has a Ways
to Go to Get to No. 1." *Financial Post*, April 9, 2021.
https://financialpost.com/executive/executivesummary/
posthaste-shopifys-tobi-lutke-is-canadas-second-richest-
person-but-he-has-a-ways-to-go-toget-to-no-1.

Williams, Roy, and Vic Preisser. 2010. *Preparing Heirs: Five
Steps to a Successful Transition of Family Wealth and
Values*. Bandon, OR: Robert D. Reed Publishers.

Wilmouth, Brad. 2010. "Mick Jagger Recounts Fleeing
High Tax Rates in England, Success 'Resented' Unlike
in America." Newsbusters, May 21, 2010. https://
newsbusters.org/blogs/nb/bradwilmouth/2010/05/21/
mick-jagger-recounts-fleeing-high-tax-rates-england-
success.

Wilton, Katherine. 2018. "Concordia's First Female Building
Engineer Gifts $15M to Alma Mater." *Montreal Gazette*,
September 24, 2018. https://montrealgazette.com/news/
local-news/concordias-first-femalebuilding-
engineer-gifts-15m-to-alma-mater.

The World Bank. n.d. "The World Bank in China." The World Bank. Accessed September 4, 2021. www.worldbank.org/en/country/china/overview.

Worthwhile Canadian Initiative. 2008. "Canada and Argentina in the 20th Century." Worthwhile Canadian Initiative (blog). https://worthwhile.typepad.com/worthwhile_canadian_initi/2008/04/canada-and-arge.html.

Yakabuski, Konrad. 2021. "Postpandemic Ottawa Should Heed Robert Mundell's Warnings on Taxes." *The Globe and Mail*, April 7, 2021.

Zagorsky, Jay L. 2018. "How Winning $1.54 Billion in Mega Millions Could Still Lead to Bankruptcy." *The Conversation*, October 19, 2018. https://theconversation.com/how-winning-1-54-billion-in-megamillions-could-still-lead-to-bankruptcy-105275.

Zeballos-Roig, Joseph. 2019. "4 European Countries Still Have a Wealth Tax. Here's How Much Success They've Each Had." Business Insider, November 7, 2019. www.businessinsider.com/4-european-countries-wealth-tax-spain-norway-switzerland-belgium-2019-11.

INDEX

Cardozo, Robin, 103
Carnegie Foundation, 113
Cato Institute, 36
C.D. Howe Institute, 72–73
Centre for Addiction and Mental
  Health (CAMH), 100, 115
CEO compensation, 33–35
Chang, Raymond G., 117–118
Chávez, Hugo, 44
Clinton, Bill, 34, 69, 132
Cody, Gina Parvaneh, 52–53
Community Food Centres
  Canada, 115
compensation, CEO
  government legislation of,
    34
  performance pay, 34
  ratio to worker's pay, 33
  tax deductibility cap, 34
COVID-19
  arts and culture, effects on,
    113
  business, effect on, 60
  deficit-to-GDP, Canada, 135
  economy, effect on, 39–40
  health care system, effect
    on, 108
  philanthropic contributions,
    during, 115
Cross, Philip, 74, 79, 80, 81

D
Dancers for Cancer, 125
Depardieu, Gérard, 77
Disney, Walt, 63
Dousmanis-Curtis, Alex, 51
Dyson, James, 9

E
economic freedom, four pillars
  of, 42
Economic Policy Institute, 33
education, philanthropic
  donations to, 101, 110–112
Edwards, Chris, 36
Elgar, Frank, 68

Ewing Marion Kauffman
  Foundation, 62

F
Fannie Mae bailout, 29
Fichtner, Larry, 22–23
financial crises, 2008
  Fannie Mae bailout, 29
  Freddie Mac bailout, 29
  Greece, debt crises, 134
  Occupy movement, 30–31
  Piketty theory, 31–32
  ProPublica bailout tracker,
    29–30
  protests against, bailouts, 30
  return on bailout
    investment, 30
  Troubled Asset Relief
    Program (TARP), 29
  US government action, 29
financial crises, Canada 1990s,
  134
"five dollar day" 1914, 63
five forces of prosperity, 127
Food Banks Canada, 115
Ford, Henry, 62–63
four pillars of economic
  freedom, 42
fourth industrial revolution, 129
Francis, Diane, 85–87
Fraser Institute's Canadian
  Consumer Tax Index, 42
Freddie Mac bailout, 29
free enterprise system, 41–42,
  43, 45, 127
Fregin, Doug, 55–57
full income poverty measure,
  40

G
Gates, Bill, 3, 55, 100, 101
Ghert, Bernie, 86
Gilgan, Peter, 109–110
Gladstone and Maisie Chang
  Chair in Teaching of Internal
  Medicine, 118
global GDP, 42

global poverty, reduction in,
41–44
government role, wealth
creation
    capitalism, encouragement
        of, 24, 136–137
    diversification, business
        ownership, 87
    executive pay packages,
        legislation for, 33–34
    fair playing field, equal
        opportunity, 5, 129
    free market, encouragement,
        5
    industrial revolutions, 129
    infrastructure, reliability of,
        130–131
    open trade, 133
    spending, into debt,
        134–135
    taxes, maintain global
        competitiveness, 132

H
Hartford, Huntington, 92–93
health care, philanthropic
    donations to, 108–110
health care spending, 108
Henderson, David R., 41, 45
Heritage Foundation, 42, 45
Hollande, François, 76–77
Hoover Institution, 41
Hospital for Sick Children, 125
Hurun Global Rich List, 47
Hyde, Tom, 82

I
IHS Markit, 99
immigrant, wealth creators,
    51–53, 61–62, 86–87
income tax, 32, 42, 73–75, 78
Index of Economic Freedom, 42
inequality, wealth. *See* wealth
    gap
infrastructure, importance of,
    130–131
inheritance tax, 84–85

inherited wealth
    average life expectancy
        of family business, 90–91
    decline of, in Canada, 85–87
    effect of government policy
        on, 87
    entrepreneurial drive, and,
        91
    family dynamics and, 89–91
    historical concentration of,
        85–86
    new immigrants and, 87
    old money vs. new money,
        87
    paternalism, 90
    public sector impact, 86–87
    retaining money, difficulties
        of, 92–93
    role of chartered banks,
        85–86
    taxation on, 84–85
    wealth retention and failure
        of future generations,
        87–89, 92–93
International Monetary Fund,
    133

J
Jackman, Hal, 103
Jaffe, Dennis, 90
Johnson, Donald K., 102–105
Johnson, Lyndon, 37–38, 40

K
Kalanick, Travis, 65
Kennedy, John, F., 37
Knight, Phil, 63

L
Lankin, Frances, 104
Lazaridis, Mike, 55–57
Lessons Learned on Bay Street,
    102
Losing the Signal, 57
lottery ticket winnings, 91
low income cut-off (LICO), 40
Lululemon, 54
Lütke, Tobias, 52

DEREK BULLEN is Founder and CEO of S.i. Systems ULC, one of the largest professional services companies in Canada, with thousands of information technology (IT) consultants working on projects for blue-chip corporations and government agencies across Canada. He is the author of *High Velocity*, a book to help new professionals in IT develop their soft business skills.

Experiencing life is a large part of Derek's purpose, from vision quests with the Goodstriker family of the Blood Nation in Southern Alberta, to multiple Camino pilgrimages across Spain, and to many visits to Sri Narayani Peedam in Malakodai, India. Derek continually refreshes the way forward for himself and his company by growing from the inside.

Derek and his wife and three children split their time between homes in Calgary and Vancouver.